HANDBOOK II

ADVANCED TEACHING STRATEGIES FOR ADJUNCT FACULTY

Revised Third Edition

Donald E. Greive, Ed.D.

Editor

To Order, contact:

The Part-Time Press
P.O. Box 130117
Ann Arbor, MI 48113-0117
1(734)930-6854
FAX: 1(734)665-9001

First printing: November, 2000

© *2006 The Part-Time Press, Inc.*

Library of Congress Data
Catalog Card Number:

ISBN: 0-940017-26-1 (paperback)
ISBN: 0-940017-27-X (hardcover)

Printed in the United States of America

Table of Contents

Acknowledgments

While the contributions of all who provided support for *Handbook II: Advanced Teaching Strategies for Adjunct Faculty* can not be recognized, special mention of those who contributed extensively in their time and energies is in order.

I am indebted first and foremost to the authors who have provided their expertise so that others in the profession may benefit. They are: TinnieA. Banks, Sheri Bidwell, Helen Burnstad, Hikmat Chedid, AnitaC.R. Gorham, JosephC. Gorham, M.B. McKinley, Michael Parsons, Andrea Peck, Arlene Sego, Kay Stephan and Elizabeth Tice. I am also indebted to the staffs at The Teaching & Learning Center at the University of Nebraska and *Inside Iowa State* at Iowa State University.

I would also like to thank the following people for allowing the use of their permission to reprint their Classroom Applications article in the final section. They are Tinnie Banks, Cameron Chambers, LisaLend Cohen, SwenandJoLynnAutry DiGranes, MaryAlice Griffin and Donnie McGahee, Rea Kirk, Charles Schmidtke, Harolyn Sharpe, John Stoebig, Eileen Teare, Darcy Wakefield, and Cheryl Welch.

On a personal note, I wish to thank Dr. Al Smith and Richard France for professional help and counsel along the way, Catherine Worden for the energies and efforts to "put it all together" and Janet Greive for counsel and assistance in manuscript preparation.

Without these people and many others this publication would not have been possible.

Don Greive
Editor

TOPIC I:

Utilizing the Techniques of Andragogy

By Donald Greive

Most full- and part-time instructors in college classrooms today were first introduced to teaching through the use of pedagogical techniques. Pedagogy, however, is based upon the teaching of children and is synonymous with the meaning of the word "leader". Thus, traditionally, teachers have been viewed as leaders in the learning process. This role involved not only the development of learning objectives, but also the development of classroom techniques and activities which are then implemented by the class "leader." In this pedagogical model the teacher had full responsibility for making all decisions about what will be learned and how it will be learned, when it will be learned and if it has been learned (Knowles, 1990).

With the changing student clientele there has emerged a need for a broader approach to the teaching/learning process. In the 1960s the average age of college students was 21; whereas recent statistics show that the average student age is 28. With the arrival of an older and more diverse student body, instructors are confronted with the task of addressing a different set of needs in the classroom. Not only do adults wish to draw upon their previous experience, but they usually come to class ready and motivated to learn. In addition, they are self-directed and may be motivated to learn for real life needs as well as self satisfaction. They are often goal-oriented and problem solvers and bring with them a need to know *why* they are learning something. This has led to the emergence of a different theory for the teaching of adults.

It is obvious from the previous description that the strategies of pedagogy (instructor-directed learning) would fall short of the needs of the modern classroom. Thus came the development of the andragogical model pioneered and adopted for use by Malcolm Knowles. Knowles based his andragogical teaching model on these newly defined characteristics of the college student which he generally calls the adult student. This andragogical model is based upon:

1. the student's need to know,
2. the learner's self concept,
3. the role of the learner's experience,
4. the readiness to learn,
5. an orientation to learning, and
6. motivation.

To accommodate the andragogical model of teaching adults or today's college student, we must again examine the motivation for adult learners. Far from just earning credits to get a degree as the major motivation, today's students and adult learners bring with them additional needs. Often the student in today's classroom will be there to meet a social need as well as an intellectual one. Many are actually striving to build competencies to assist others in their culture or simply possess a strong interest in the topic being discussed. Many adults will be responding to specific training or professional advancement needs and will have difficulty in adjusting to courses that do not specifically address that goal or activity (Knowles, 1990).

Accompanying this set of needs are an additional set of behaviors or conditions which may be barriers to learning. For the adult learner, these may include such things as: outside family responsibilities and activities, medical and rehabilitative problems, child care, transportation problems, and lack of confidence. These conditions make it doubly important for adjunct and part-time faculty to be aware of a learning process that accommodates rather than alienates students. An additional characteristic of the adult learner is that "they will vote with their feet" in terms of course value; that is, if their needs are not met, they will simply disappear. Thus the importance of the development of the andragogical model of teaching.

Andragogy has often been called the art and science of teaching adults. The driving force of this model differs from pedagogy in that it places the student at the center of the learning process and it gives emphasis to collaborative relationships among students and with the instructor. The model prescribes problem-solving activities based upon the students' need rather than the goals of the discipline or the instructor. In short, the andragogical model calls for the college teacher to become a facilitator of learning rather than a director of learning. This model is sometimes described as learner-based and learner-organized. However, one must be cautious that this does not imply that the instructor show up in class with the attitude of "what do you want to do today, gang?" In fact, the andragogical model requires more professional and quality teaching techniques and strategies than the self-directed pedagogical model.

The first step in developing andragogical teaching strategy is to create a warm and friendly classroom environment. Without open communication and a warm atmosphere, students will withdraw from the collaborative process and wait to be told what to write down so they can pass the test. Be aware that many adults are anxious about their learning experience and lack confidence, thus it is important to avoid embarrassing them or making them feel ill at ease. Activities in which the students feel confident and secure should be planned. This climate should produce a nonjudgmental atmosphere in which students share in the responsibility for their learning and are not dependent upon instructor expertise.

Important to this relationship is the first class session. The first class session will very often set the tone for the balance of the course or the program, and it should start on a healthy note. Warm and open conversation can be implemented in the first session by such activities as introductions, discussions of the goals of the course, discussions of why the students are there (with the instructor indicating why he or she is there) and the incorporation of group work or partnership. This can often be accomplished simply by eliciting a response to an ice breaker statement or a question concerning the experiences of individuals in class. It is important in the first class session that you establish yourself as a partner in learning and not the expert that has all the answers. Remember that there are many students in class who are older, less affluent, of different races, or with disabilities who have not experienced support or positive classroom behavior. It is important that these individuals are connected to the rest of the students in the class and made to feel welcome. Also, it is not unusual for students to have special needs which they do not care to verbalize publicly. All students should be invited to discuss with you privately any personal needs or considerations they may have.

Classroom Strategies

During the first class it is important to establish that although the program or course will be collaborative and cooperative, it will not be a student-run class. Make it clear, however, that classroom activities will be student-centered and not discipline-centered and that relevant participation (not irrelevant) of all students is not only welcomed but expected. Many of the techniques of andragogy are the same techniques that good instructors have been using for years. Hopefully, the day of the college instructor standing in front of a group and lecturing for an hour or more has passed.

Conducting a Discussion

Obviously, one of the most elementary and effective methods of collaborative learning is developing a stimulating discussion. This can be implemented by asking the group refreshing questions about the assignment, listing critical points concerning the assignment or related to outside assignments, and breaking the class into small groups to reach consensus. Obviously the discussion must be facilitated in such a way that it maintains class integrity and is not general conversation.

The more students that are actively involved in their learning experience the better the learning environment becomes. Active involvement can include: presentation by students of issues and questions of concern, panel presentations, and student demonstrations of their experience or knowledge that may be related to the course being taught.

Cooperative Learning

Cooperative learning is probably the most often used student-centered technique in the college classroom today. Sometimes called collaborative learning, it is actually one of the oldest educational techniques. Cooperative learning brings students with differing abilities together in small groups where they teach each other the concepts of the class by reinforcing the lecture and text materials. The students may either work on specific projects cooperatively or take selected quizzes and/or tests together. This process forces all students to become actively involved in all activities. For the instructor there are two significant prerequisites for good cooperative education groups—thorough planning and total commitment. As a facilitator, the instructor becomes an idea person and a resource person and may even be a mediator (Sego, 1996). For additional information on the use of cooperative learning techniques refer to Topic XI or the reference cited above.

Questioning

The most common activity in the traditional classroom that lends itself to the andragogical model is the formulation of good questions. Good questions can lead to active and broad student participation during the learning activity. The instructor as a facilitator reserves the right to develop such questions. A few things must be kept in mind in the development of good questions. Questions should not be posed that can be answered by simple yes or no or one-word answer, rather they are posed for the stimulation of discussion. Many times questions may require a waiting period (whether they be directed to a class or an individual) and that the allowance of a period of silence after the question is not necessarily negative. Basically there are three major types of questions:

1. **Factual Questions.** Used at appropriate times to check the background knowledge of students. These may be necessary before proceeding to the next task.

2. **Application or Interpretation Questions.** These questions should be formulated to get relationships, applications, or analysis of facts and materials.

3. **Problem Questions.** Discussion questions are used to provide students the opportunity to develop solutions to a problem or issue that may be different from that of the instructor.

A spin-off of a good questioning process will be one in which a student may ask another student or group of students for assistance in formulating an answer which could then lead to an active interaction throughout the class (McKeachie, 1994).

Non-Participating Students

The greatest fear of instructors new to the andragogical model is that students may not respond or will remain silent. The reverse of this type of conduct is that a few students may dominate the class at the expense of others. This can often be prevented by involving the students in the activities described for the first class session. That is, reduce the students' fear of speaking to build their confidence and to make them feel that they are a contributor to the class. Sometimes it is best to have students write out their answer to a posed verbal question; thus the non-participating student can be asked simply what they have written down, or if they have developed an answer with a partner, ask one for the response and ask the other if they agree. Non-participant students can be greatly encouraged by the old technique of body language. A nod of the head, a smile, or a "thanks, that's a good answer" can do wonders for a student who has never before been praised for classroom participation.

One activity, when starting the class is to have the students write a short autobiography with an option to write out a life experience they may not wish to talk about themselves but give permission to the instructor to use as a class anecdote. (Permission granted, of course).

Another technique that is effective is that of asking questions that have general answers. In this case you should feel free to call upon any student in class and accept any answer given.

Another simple but effective active technique for classroom involvement is a buzzword. In this procedure the instructor may split the class into two groups or any number of groups they wish, have them assemble and develop a hypothesis that is relevant to the course work, one application of the principle and an example of the concept.

Conclusion

To contrast the two models discussed here Knowles describes reactive and proactive learning. In the reactive environment (pedagogy), Knowles describes the traditional course instructor as requiring the students to respect their authority, to commit to learning as a means to an end, to develop competitive relationships that require only the skills and the ability to listen uncritically, to retain information, to take notes, and to predict exam questions. Whereas the proactive (andragogical) instructional environment would include people with intellectual curiosity, the spirit of inquiry, knowledge of resources available, healthy skepticism toward authority and expertise, criteria for testing, commitment to learning which requires the ability to formulate questions answerable by data, the ability to identify data available by printed material, ability to scan quickly, ability to test data against criteria, reliability and validity and the ability to analyze data to produce answers to questions (Knowles, 1990).

References

Knowles, M. (1990). *The adult learner-A neglected species.* Houston, TX. Gulf Publishing Co.

McKeachie, W., et. al. (1994). *Teaching tips.* Lexington, MA. D. C. Heath and Co.

Sego, A. (1994). *Cooperative learning-A classroom guide.* Elyria, OH. Info-Tec.

Dr. Don Greive is author/editor and consultant for adjunct faculty programs.

TOPIC II:

The Modern Student

By Donald Greive

Much has been written in recent years concerning the modern college student in comparison to the "traditional college student". Other than a significant age difference, however, the question may be raised, "Is there really a significant difference between today's students and those of former years?"

Some describe the modern student as "The Generation Y Student" or "Y-Gens" with insinuations of behavioral differences. Others say that such a label is no more definitive than trying to define a teenager and to stereotype them as a single group. Those that dwell on the Generation Y concept describe the students as often bored and unmotivated, having an "attitude" toward college and resistant to disciplined study. They maintain that it is difficult to maintain their attention and with their desire for immediate gratification, to establish meaningful learning objectives and goals.

The counter argument maintains that these students were always present in all classrooms through all generations. Other than the age difference, other characteristics of the Y-Generation Student are that they have experienced fantasy driven by television; selected without guidance their own movies, videos, and music; and have grown up surrounded by the influences of media. They have lived in the world of media entertainment and with the advent of the Internet have experienced a cultural environment that appears unmonitored. This environment has led to attitudes that may surface in the classroom in the form of consumer expectations and lack of respect for authority. It appears that this is a cultural behavior rather than an educational one.

In fact, on occasion these types of attitudes are expressed in confrontational rather than cooperative behavior. Although one should not err on the side of generalizing about today's college classes, it should be recognized that the cultural factors influencing the students are often different that those of a few years ago. Many of the students today are the first generation known as "latch key kids" who grew up with both parents working. Many were raised in single-parent homes with a fast food mentality and are the product of divorces. These facts are presented here as a reminder of the need to provide special consideration and assistance to all students, some of which may fall into this category.

Classroom Implications

Realizing the challenges presented by today's students, as a part-time instructor, you should be cognizant of the fact that you need to build teaching strategies and procedures that will activate the learner. Such activities include role playing and cooperative education strategies described elsewhere in this book. It should be kept in mind that today's students will expect a certain amount of autonomy and will respond to classroom activities that they see as meaningful and in which they are involved. They will probably respond to topics and work assignments that may be researched and investigated on the Internet rather than in print documents and periodicals from the library. In terms of immediate gratification, they will expect answers to their questions in class and comments and notes on their tests and quizzes.

Planning Classroom Activities

It is important that when teaching the modern day student that you keep in mind that these students want to *do* something rather than *know* something. Materials for class presentations should be designed to incorporate a variety of formats including charts, videos, graphics, and even PowerPoint™ presentations. In the formulation of class objectives and activities, it is not suggested that you forfeit your role; it is suggested, however, that students could be involved in describing and selecting some of the activities that they will perform in order to reach those objectives. It is important that when teaching the Y-Generation student that you remember that you are a facilitator of learning and not the final expert.

Teaching Tips for the Modern Student

As indicated earlier in this discussion there are significant forces at work in our environment and culture which effect the behavior of today's students. Although many of the traditional teaching strategies still apply, it remains that teaching is teaching and learning is learning. With changing attitudes and cultural influences, however, you will occasionally find yourself in a situation that is particularly challenging. Listed below are some of these situations as they relate to the modern classroom.

The Aggressive Student

Aggressive students are common in the modern classroom. The modern student will not hesitate to speak up, to question why certain things must be learned, how it's going to help, and why they should do it. Many times the response that "this is a course requirement" is not sufficient. The initial response, of course, is to meet the aggressive student in an informal atmosphere during a break to try to break down barriers and direct the energies to the real purpose at hand—to assist the student in being successful in the course. If it is a particular issue in which there is sharp disagreement, you must state your position calmly and rationally and recognize that not everyone agrees with everyone else in the class, including the instructor. This can also be turned into a very positive learning experience involving the aggressive student by presenting the issues to the class by simply saying "how do the rest of you feel about this?" This can very effectively be used as an interactive tool in the classroom where small groups can meet to discuss the issues and reach a conclusion.

The Class Expert

With the increased numbers of adults returning to higher education, many students in class may be older than the instructor and there will sometimes be situations where a class expert will surface. These students typically fall into two categories: a) the genuine expert who may in fact know more about a particular topic or issue than the instructor (this is very easy to accommodate by inviting the student to make a presentation) and b) the "know-it-all" student who feels he or she is an expert on anything at anytime. Dealing with this student sometimes leads to an argument rather than a discussion and needs to be minimized or it will distract the class. The easiest way to handle such behavior is to allow the student to express him or herself, and ask the other students for response and reaction. This will usually convey the message that his or her contribution is either of value or is wasting their time.

The final responsibility still lies with the instructor to point out the objectives of the course and to get on with the business of the class.

The Inattentive Student

The inattentive student can take many forms. Occasionally it will be a group of two or three students who carry on their own conversation at their own pace. Occasionally it will be the student who sits with a blank facial expression as if to dare you to teach them. Many times they will respond to questions with the answer "I don't know".

To counter this behavior, several techniques are available.

The first is a buzz session group where students are put together and each are asked to participate. If this does not work, the instructor may ask each student in the class to write a short paper indicating what they have observed over the last half hour of class and what they would like to see discussed. A relocation of the seating arrangement may also be effective. Finally, you must realize that a few students cannot be allowed to usurp the learning opportunities of the other students in the class. Remember the X-Generation students consider themselves consumers and customers and they expect the product to be delivered regardless of the situation.

The Discouraged Student

Possibly the most important student for the instructor of X Generation is the student that is discouraged, insecure, and/or not confident of their ability to succeed even before they enter the classroom. You must realize that this is not the result of your behavior, of your class preparation, or of your making. These are the students referred to in the previous discussion that may have been recently divorced, have had a serious illness or death in the family, have medical or disability problems or a number of other problems to face. Years ago these people would not have been in college classrooms, and today they are arriving with the hope that there is some value and benefit to this experience in their lives. Anyone who has taught in the modern classroom has experienced the success stories of this type of students. Many times they are difficult to identify because of denial. The only sure method that you can incorporate to include these people is to make sure that all students are treated with the utmost respect and support and that you have an arsenal of professional techniques to address and encourage these and all students.

Dr. Don Greive is author/editor and consultant for adjunct faculty programs.

TOPIC III:

Focus on ... 101 Things You Can Do the First Three Weeks of Class

Beginnings are important. Whether it is a large introductory class for freshmen or an advanced course in a major field, it makes good sense to start the semester off well. Students will decide very early – some say the first day of class – whether they will like the course, its contents, the teacher, and their fellow students.

The following list of "101 Things You Can Do..." is offered in the spirit of starting off right. It is a catalog of suggestions for college teachers who are looking for fresh ways of creating the best possible environment for learning. Not just the first day, but the first three weeks of a course are especially important, studies say, in retaining capable students. Even if a syllabus is printed and lecture notes are ready to go the week before class, most college teachers can usually make adjustments in teaching methods as the course unfolds and the characteristics of their students become known.

These suggestions have been gathered from college and university faculty at several institutions. For many faculty, much of this is "old hat." But even for long-time teachers, there may be that one jewel of a suggestion that may help get you off on the right foot. The rationale for these methods is based on the following needs:

> ❧ **To help students make the transition** from high school and, in August, summer activities to learning in college;

   • **To direct students' attention** to the immediate situation for learning – the hour in the classroom;

   • **To spark intellectual curiosity** – to challenge students;

   • **To support beginners** and neophytes in the process of learning in the discipline;

   • **To encourage the students' active involvement** in learning; and

   • **To build a sense of community** in the classroom.

Here, then, are some ideas for college teachers to use in their courses at the beginning of the term.

Helping Students Make Transitions

1. **Hit the ground running** on the first day of class with substantial content.

2. **Take attendance**: roll call, clipboard, sign in, seating chart.

3. **Introduce teaching assistants** by slide, short presentation, or self-introduction.

4. **Hand out** an informative, artistic, and user-friendly **syllabus.**

5. **Give an assignment** on the first day to be collected at the next meeting.

6. **Start laboratory experiments** and other exercises the first time lab meets.

7. **Call attention (written and oral) to what makes good lab practice**: completing work to be done, procedures, equipment, clean up, maintenance, safety, conservation of supplies, full use of lab time.

8. **Give a learning style inventory** to help students find out about themselves.

9. If your campus has one, **direct students to the Academic Success Center** for help on basic skills.

10. **Tell students how much time they will need to study** for this course.

11. **Hand out supplemental study aids**: library use, study tips, supplemental readings and exercises.

12. **Explain how to study** for the kind of tests you give.

13. **Put in writing a limited number of ground rules** regarding absence, late work, testing procedures, grading, and general decorum, and maintain these.

14. **Announce office hours** frequently and hold them without fail.

15. **Show students how to handle learning in large classes** and impersonal situations.

16. **Give sample test questions.**

17. **Give sample test answers.**

18. **Explain the difference between legitimate collaboration and academic dishonesty**; be clear when collaboration is wanted and when it is forbidden.

19. **Seek out a different student each day** and get to know something about him or her.

20. **Ask students to write about what important things** are currently going on in their lives.

21. **Find out about students' jobs**: if they are working, how many hours a week, and what kind of jobs they hold.

Directing Students' Attention

22. **Greet students at the door** when they enter the classroom.

23. **Start class on time.**

24. **Make a grand stage entrance** to hush a large class and gain attention.

25. **Give a pre-test** on the day's topic.

26. **Start the lecture with a puzzle, question, paradox,**

picture, or cartoon on slide or transparency to focus the day's topic.

27. **Elicit student questions and concerns** at the beginning of the class and list these on the chalkboard to be answered during the hour.

28. **Have students write down what they think the important issues** or key points on the day's lecture will be.

29. **Ask the person who is reading the student newspaper what is in the news today.**

Challenging Students

30. **Have students write out their expectations** for the course and their goals for learning.

31. **Use variety in methods of presentation** every class meeting.

32. **Stage a figurative "coffee break"** about 20 minutes into the hour: tell an anecdote, invite students to put down their pens and pencils, refer to a current event, shift media.

33. **Incorporate community resources**: plays, concerts, the State Fair, government agencies, businesses, the outdoors.

34. **Show a film in a novel way**: stop it for discussion, show a few frames only, anticipate the ending, hand out a viewing or critique sheet, play and replay parts.

35. **Share your philosophy of teaching** with your students.

36. **Form a student panel** to present alternative views of the same concept.

37. **Stage a "change-your-mind" debate,** with students moving to different parts of the classroom to signal change in opinion during the discussion.

38. **Conduct a "living" demographic survey** by having the students move to different parts of the classroom: size of high schools, rural vs. urban, consumer preferences.

39. **Tell about your current research interests** and how you got there from your own beginnings in the discipline.

40. **Conduct a role-play** to make a point or lay out issues.

41. **Let your students assume the role of a professional** in the discipline: philosopher, literary critic, biologist, agronomist, political scientist, engineer.

42. **Conduct idea-generating and brainstorming sessions** to expand horizons.

43. **Give students two passages of material containing alternative views** to compare and contrast.

44. **Distribute a list of the unsolved problems**, dilemmas, or great questions in your discipline and invite students to claim one as their own to investigate.

45. **Ask students what books they read** over the summer.

46. **Ask students what is going on in the state legislature** on a subject which may affect their future.

47. **Let your students see the enthusiasm** you have for your subject and your love of learning.

48. **Take students with you** to hear guest speakers or special programs on campus.

49. **Plan a "scholar-gypsy" lesson** or unit which shows students the excitement of discovery in your discipline.

Providing Support

50. **Collect students' current telephone numbers and addresses** and let them know that you may need to reach them.

51. **Check out absentees.** Call or write a personal note.

52. **Diagnose the students' prerequisite learning** by a questionnaire or pre-test and give them feedback as soon as possible.

53. **Hand out study questions** and study guides.

54. **Be redundant.** Students should hear, read, and see key materials at least three times.

55. **Allow students to demonstrate progress in learning**: summary quiz over the day's work, a written reaction to the day's material.

56. **Use non-graded feedback** to let students know how they are doing: post answers to ungraded quizzes and problem sets, exercises in class, verbal feedback.

57. **Reward behavior you want**: praise, stars, honor roll, personal note.

58. **Use a light touch**: smile, tell a good joke, break test anxiety with a sympathetic comment.

59. **Organize.** Give visible structure by posting the day's "menu" on the chalkboard or overhead.

60. **Use multiple media**: overhead, slides, film, videotape, audio tape, models, sample material.

61. **Use multiple examples, in multiple media**, to illustrate key points and important concepts.

62. **Make appointments** with all students (individually or in small groups).

63. **Hand out wallet-sized telephone cards** with all important telephone numbers listed: office, department, resource centers, teaching assistant, lab.

64. **Print all important course dates** on a card that can be handed out and taped to a mirror.

65. **Eavesdrop on students before and after class** and join their conversations about course topics.

66. **Maintain an open lab grade book**, with grades kept current, during lab time so that students can check their progress.

67. **Check to see if any students are having problems** with any academic or campus matters and direct those who are to appropriate offices or resources.

68. Tell students what they need to do to receive an "A" in your course.

69. **Stop the world to find out** what your students are thinking, feeling, and doing in their everyday lives.

Encouraging Active Learning

70. Have students write something.

71. **Have students keep a three-week three-times-a-week journal** in which they comment, ask questions, and answer questions about course topics.

72. **Invite students to critique each other's essays or short answer questions** on tests for readability or content.

73. **Invite students to ask questions** and wait for the response.

74. **Probe student responses** to question their comments.

75. **Put students into pairs or "learning cells"** to quiz each other over material for the day.

76. **Give students an opportunity** to voice opinions about the subject matter.

77. **Have students apply subject matter** to solve real problems.

78. **Give students red, yellow, and green cards** (made of posterboard) and periodically call for a vote on an issue by asking for a simultaneous show of cards.

79. **Roam the aisles of a large classroom** and carry on running conversations with students as they work on course problems (a portable microphone helps.)

80. **Ask a question directed to one student** and wait for an answer.

81. **Place a suggestion box** in the rear of the room and encourage students to make written comments every time the class meets.

82. **Do oral "show-of-hands" multiple-choice tests** for summary, review, and instant feedback.

83. **Use task groups** to accomplish specific objectives.

84. **Grade quizzes and exercises in class** as a learning tool.

85. **Give students plenty of opportunity for practice** before a major test.

86. **Give a test early in the semester** and return it graded in the next class meeting.

87. **Have students write questions** on index cards to be collected and answered the next class period.

88. **Make collaborative assignments** for several students to work together on.

89. **Assign written paraphrases and summaries** of difficult reading.

90. **Give students a take-home problem** relating to the day's lecture.

91. **Encourage students to bring current news items** to class which relate to the subject matter and post these on a bulletin board nearby.

Building Community

92. **Learn names.** Everyone makes an effort to learn at least a few names.

93. **Set up a buddy system** so students can contact each other about assignments and coursework.

94. **Find out about your students** via questions on an index card.

95. **Take pictures of students** (snapshots in small groups, mug shots) and post in classroom, office or lab.

96. **Arrange helping trios of students** to assist each other in learning and growing.

97. **Form small groups for getting acquainted;** mix and

form new groups several times.

98. **Assign a team project early in the semester** and provide time to assemble the team.

99. **Help students form study groups** to operate outside the classroom.

100. **Solicit suggestions from students** for outside resources
and guest speakers on course topics.

Feedback on Teaching

101. **Gather student feedback** in the first three weeks of the semester to improve teaching and learning.

Printed with permission, Teaching and Learning Center, University of Nebraska, Lincoln, NE.

TOPIC IV:

Developing the Environment for Learning

By Helen Burnstad

Change is rapidly altering the face of post-secondary education. Technology, increased competition, more student demands, accountability efforts, and consumerism have generated a reconsideration of the teaching/learning enterprise. Within the past five years, the Learning College movement has advocated a change of focus in the classroom—from the focus on the teacher delivering content to the student learning it. This change of focus has caused many faculty members, administrators, and staff developers to consider what elements create a classroom climate that encourages more student responsibility for learning. Student needs and interests are considered as mindfully as teacher attitudes. In order to create a learning environment four areas should be examined:

1. teachers' expectations,
2. teacher and teaching behaviors,
3. physical classroom space, and
4. strategies used to create the environment for learning.

Teacher Expectations

Each teacher should have a clear picture of his or her own style and expectations. A variety of recommendations can be found in the literature. On the one hand, writers recommend that you know your own learning style, using whichever learning style instrument you select—the 4-Mat system, Kolb, Dunn or others—since your learning style most likely contributes to choices you make about how to teach. Others suggest you know your work behavioral style, determined by using a learning tool such as the Personal Profile System from Carlson Learning Company, or your personality type using the Myers-Briggs Type Indicator. These many tools will help you be clearer about your teaching style. Student feedback may also be a way of gaining insight into your style.

Recent attention has been given to teaching as a "calling" or "art" rather than a science. Parker Palmer in his book, *The Courage to Teach*,

> takes teachers on an inner journey toward re-connecting with their vocation and their students—and recovering their passion for one of the most difficult and important of human endeavors. "This book builds on a simple premise: good teaching cannot be reduced to technique, good teaching comes from the identity and integrity of the teacher" (cover flap, 1998).

Teachers need to know themselves and their style.

A second area to consider is the teacher's teaching goals. Using the "Teaching Goals Inventory and Self-Scorable Worksheet" (Angelo & Cross, 1993, pp. 393-397), a faculty member can reflect on his or her purposes for the course. This information helps to frame your philosophy and intent regarding the content of the course.

Once a faculty member has given consideration to the dimensions of both art and goals, the challenge is to present your expectations to your students. Students want and need to know their teacher and their teacher's passion for the subject area. As a faculty member, share that information with your students!

Teacher Behavior

Classroom climate includes your presence in the classroom. Students want to know if you love your subject area — why? how?—as well as know that you like them. A pleasant persona is helpful. Enthusiasm demonstrated through energetic and engaging activities are desirable as well.

It goes without saying that preparation is paramount in communicating expectations to students. Be clear about your belief in them and their capability of learning the information in your class. You are a "significant other" for your students. If you communicate an expectation that the class will be wonderful, the learning will be engaging, and you'll all work hard together, you have established an expectation that your students will strive to meet. On the other hand, if you present them with an expectation of difficulty and predict that one half of them will fail the course, you've set their expectations as well. Being positive serves as a motivator for students.

Your expectations should also extend to how you wish your students to interact with one another. If you intend to use cooperative learning structures or team work, being clear about your expectations of the students is also important.

You may extend your expectations by explaining your teaching philosophy. What do you want your students to learn? How will you help them be successful? How does your classroom look "different" from other classrooms?

Classroom Arrangement

The classroom you have been assigned may dictate how flexible you can be with the seating, the focus of attention, or the use of technology. If you are in a fixed-seat room, you will have to work within some confines but even that should not deter you from using variety in your classroom. Application of an understanding of learning principles such as attention span, need for change of focus, reinforcement, time on task, and processing strategies should encourage you to ask students to move, interact, ask questions, respond to one another, work quietly on tasks, listen respectfully to each other, and challenge assumptions.

Classroom Strategies for Creating Climate

- ➷ **Arrange the classroom to establish eye contact** between and among students and you. A circle or horseshoe will work nicely.

- ➷ **Introduce yourself to your students.** Be sure they know who you are, what the class is, why you are teaching the course, what background you bring to the classroom, how excited you are to share the semester with them. Make them feel comfortable and welcome.

- ➷ Be prepared for the possibility of **having students of very diverse backgrounds.** Capitalize on age differences. Mix groups so older students are with younger ones; non-native speakers of English are with native speakers, races are mixed or ability levels are combined.

- ➷ **The more actively involved students are** from the very first meeting, the better the chance of having students become comfortable in your classroom and expect to continue to be active.

- ➷ **Use a strategy for getting to know your students.** A 5" x 8" note card works very well to have students tell you about themselves. Questions might include what their major is, why they are taking the class, what their goals are for the class, what grade they intend to earn. You might also use this strategy to uncover any concerns they may have about the class, their history or past experience with the subject area, or if they are in need of any type of accommodation.

- ➷ **Take a picture of each of your students** so that you can attach it to the information card. This will also help you learn your students' names.

≈ **Learn each student's name**. Ask them what they would like to be called in class. The name on the roster may not be the name they go by. Be open to that information. Learn to pronounce the names of students correctly. Foreign names may be a special challenge but do all you can to learn each name.

≈ **Provide ways for students to get to know one another.** Use name tags, name plates, a roster, a "get acquainted" activity or two, or dyadic interviews and introductions.

≈ **Prepare a complete and lively syllabus**. Include in your syllabus a statement of your teaching philosophy, or your expectations of them, or a statement of civility and behavior, or a statement of respect, or all of the above!

≈ **Share with students how you visualize their role in the class.** Perhaps have students establish the ground rules for the class. They will include in the ground rules the same things you would say, i.e. come prepared, come on time, be open to sharing with others, be respectful, listen carefully, and other expectations for a good learning environment.

≈ **Have your students from a previous class "Leave a Legacy".** Ask students to write a letter or set of recommendations to your students for the next semester. The students will tell the new class everything they have learned about being successful in your class. Their voice will convey the need to be prepared, keep up with the assignments, follow directions, read, and interact. These Legacies serve to remove the "heavy handed" sound of some requirements from your mouth. You will be encouraged by what students say!

≈ **Use Classroom Assessment Techniques (CATs)** to continually get feedback from your students. "The One Minute Paper" or "Muddiest Point" strategies will keep the communication flowing between you and your students.

- ✎ **If you ask for feedback, feed the information back to them**. If they ask questions, respond to them. A "no" is better than no response.

- ✎ **Invite students to confer with you early and often**. Set up a system of e-mail contact. Be sure they know your office hours. You may even design a strategy where they must come to see you in your office.

- ✎ **Maintain an open grade book policy**. Student should know how they are doing in your class throughout the semester.

- ✎ **Give students opportunities for input into the course**. How can they share readings, videos, Internet sites, or other resources that could contribute to the content of the course? Encourage them to learn your subject matter outside of class. And apply it!

- ✎ **Be alert to how students are responding**. Read non-verbal feedback as much as possible. If you are engaged and sensitive, students will mirror that behavior as well.

- ✎ **Be confident in your role**. You are the content expert, that is why you were hired to teach this class.

- ✎ **Have fun!**

What you want to do to develop the environment for learning is create the classroom climate which motivates students to learn your content. These recommendations will help you do that. Consider your expectations, your philosophy, your physical setting, and the strategies you wish to use to ensure your students' success. Your students will live up—or down—to your expectations.

References

Angelo, T. A. & Cross, K. P. (1993*). Classroom assessment techniques a handbook for college teachers.* San Francisco: Jossey-Bass Publishers.

Creating a positive learning environment. (1998) Toronto: Humber College of Applied Arts and Technology.

Davis, B. G. (1993). *Tools for teaching.* San Francisco: Jossey-Bass Publishers.

McKeachie, W. J. et. al. (1994). *Teaching tips strategies, research, and theory for college and university teachers.* Lexington, MA: D. C. Heath and Company.

Palmer, P. J. (1998). *The courage to teach exploring the inner landscape of a teacher's life.* San Francisco: Jossey-Bass Publishers.

Dr. Helen Burnstad is the Director of Staff Development, Johnson County Community College, Overland Park, KS.

TOPIC V:

Connecting with the Adult Learner

By Anita C. R. Gorham and Joseph C. Gorham

Why am I here ... at this place ... at this time? Many of us have asked this question at some point in our lives. The adult learner is no exception. While most times the question is more global, many adult learners are focusing on "why am I in college at this time in my life?" While the reasons may be as varied as the cultural backgrounds and experiences of the adult learner, the answers for all will fall into one or two categories: career advancement/maintenance or self fulfillment.

As an educator of the adult learner, it is a part of our responsibility as facilitator to understand who is our student. Unlike the traditional student, they have made many life choices which have broadened their experiential base, resulting in their current educational pursuit. In many cases, their need may overshadow their values. Their values may dictate that family is first, my children should be the priority; however, because of my responsibilities, I must work and my employer is mandating that I get a degree. Many are in a constant state of juggling responsibilities and attempting to be all things to many people and entities. Their priority may very well NOT be school, but again their need has become the priority: the need to stay in the race, the need to maintain their position of provider, the need to be a role model and encourage their children.

You're no doubt saying to yourself, "this all sounds very familiar, but what does it have to do with me? How does knowing this assist me in connecting effectively with the adult learner?" While it is true the adult learner may not know all the theory behind their experiences, it in no way diminishes the fact that they have had these experiences. It is our responsibility as facilitators to develop a style of integrating practicality with the theoretical aspects of learning.

Adults are motivated to invest in higher education for a myriad of reasons. Whatever the individual reasons, importance is placed on the application of the concept and not the concept itself. Because their value system is already established, the information must be presented in a manner that allows them room to integrate it into their conceptual truth.

What you see is not necessarily what you get. Because of their many experiences, responsibilities and perceptions, the adult learner is reluctant to take unnecessary risk. In most cases, their egos are well entrenched as well as their need to be in control. They have "tried and true" behavior that has helped them assimilate and thus be accepted. We, as the facilitator, must create a "safe environment" that will encourage a respectful participatory exchange. We must balance respect of the student's experiences while maintaining control over the process. This necessitates that our egos are secure! We must be willing to take the risk of being challenged, thus relinquishing some control to gain more control. We must understand that they, like us, are a composite of their culture, gender and experience.

Many minority adult learners enter the educational arena from an experiential base that has been tried and tested by racism. Hence, it is important for the facilitator to be cognizant and sensitive to this reality. Viewed from this perspective, it can be said that many minority adult learners enter the classroom "sensitive" to and "expecting" to encounter some form of "institutionally structured racism." How the minority student copes with his or her place in an educational arena that is "perceived" as being racist or potentially racist or supporting racism, is to a degree contingent upon how aware and sensitive the facilitator is to the issue. In general, sensitivity is the ability to perceive with some accuracy what others think and feel.

In an effort to be sensitive to and empathetic toward the minority adult learner on the issues of race, it is essential that the facilitator not approach the issue by suggesting mundane and inappropriate solutions like these:

- Minorities deserve more gains than they have attained, but because gains come at the cost of others, it is unlikely that more will be forthcoming.

- Being aware of how changing standards for the sake of educating minorities is detrimental to non-minorities.

- Although inequities exist, minorities must move to clean their own slate rather than wait for institutions to provide for them; i.e. the "boot strap approach."

- Suggesting that race issues are a result of difficulties and misunderstandings stemming from diminished and poor communication, as opposed to focusing on the possibility of racism being part of the value system that serves the purpose of the individual purporting some aspect of racism.

It is imperative that facilitators realize that a certain number of minority students will enter the classroom with a perspective that has been structured by past and current experiences of racism (or what appears to them to be racism). Hence, in an effort to address the "real" or "perceived perspectives", it is necessary for the facilitator to have the ability to sense what a student might feel, verbalize, and ultimately act upon.

The following represent some aspects of sensitivity that facilitators might want to be aware of:

- How and in what manner a facilitator makes favorable or unfavorable ratings of others.

- One's ability to suspend judgment, not jump to conclusions and demonstrate the ability to be objective from one situation to another.

- The ability to feel and communicate empathy and at the same time, keep the facilitator/student relationship clear.

- ❧ Possessing a clear understanding of personality traits.

- ❧ Through accurate observation, stereotyping is avoided.

How can we as facilitators make the connection? While there are many roads to the same destination, the following represent some highlights of our collective 20 years' experience teaching the adult learner:

- ❧ **Teach where your students are.** Because of their accumulated experience, adults are generally sensitive, goal oriented, highly motivated and self directed. Be aware of the psychological, emotional, cultural and career locale of the student.

- ❧ **What's in it for me?** Material and delivery style must be viewed by the adult learner as relevant and have immediate utilitarian value.

- ❧ **Is it safe?** The facilitator must structure an environment that is adult learner friendly in all aspects of the process.

- ❧ **Teach others as you would want to be taught.** The adult learner wants to be respected, validated and would like to view the facilitator as being objective.

- ❧ **Learning, like life, is what you make of it.** The facilitator must motivate the adult learner to be an active, responsible participant in their learning process.

Anita C. R. Gorham is the Associate Director for Executive and Professional Development, Part-time Faculty and Faculty mentor, Central Michigan University, Troy, MI.
Joseph C. Gorham is a part-time faculty member at Central Michigan University, guest lecturer at several universities in the Metropolitan Detroit area, and Director of Clinical Social Work at a major Employee Assistant Program (EAP) Corporation.

TOPIC VI:

Classroom Communication

By Andrea Peck

Classroom communication involves the various means an instructor has to communicate course expectations and goals, the skills and tools used to facilitate student participation, and the actual interactions that occur between students and their teachers.

Teachers can influence how students feel about a course, their instructor, and the quality of communication that goes on in the classroom. It begins the first day of class. By arriving on time, being professionally dressed, and distributing a syllabus that documents course expectations, grading criteria, assignments, and due dates, you are not only communicating that you are prepared, organized and interested in covering the course material, but in your students' success as well. In addition, listing phone, e-mail and/or fax numbers, as well as office locations and hours lets students know when you are available outside of the classroom.

Presentation styles influence students' attitudes and performances and communicate the value you place on students and on your subject material. Being enthusiastic, animated and energetic will encourage the most unmotivated student. While presenting a lecture, establish some familiarity. Make direct eye contact, walk around the room, and directly call on students. In addition, use an assortment of visual aides—overheads, pictures, flip charts, computer graphics, handouts—examples from your life experience, and relevant information to enliven any topic and enhance your credibility and rapport.

Having clearly defined policies and procedures is a must. Students need to know when it's appropriate to ask questions, whether they can converse with others in class, and what is the appropriate protocol for arriving late, missing a class, or making up missed assignments. Not only should you document this information in your syllabus, but you'll need to reinforce it on a one-to-one basis. Problems develop when there is an inconsistent application of policies, so don't allow some students to arrive late or make up work and not extend those same privileges to everyone.

Since students come from a variety of backgrounds, experiences, and skills, learn to respect their differences. Respond directly and clearly to questions and don't patronize or condescend. It's important to reinforce the idea that learning includes experimentation and opportunities for error. And if a student requires extra time or an additional explanation, make provisions. Either meet with them after class or in a conference-style situation that will comfortably allow time for suggestions and extra assistance.

Disruptive and/or inappropriate behavior happens, so be prepared. Don't ignore anything that compromises you or your classroom. If a student is disruptive—excessively questioning, talking, or going off on a tangent—address the problem immediately. Suggest they talk with you after class, or ask them to refrain from further questions until you've completed the lecture as you're likely to cover their concerns. If the student persists, speak with them later in private about more acceptable forms of behavior.

Once you've established the groundwork for a successful classroom, you can break the ice in several ways. First, try calling directly on students to answer questions or to initiate their feedback. It encourages their involvement and sets a standard that active participation is status quo.

Use props and resources to assist those students not typically comfortable expressing themselves. The collage is an excellent tool. It uses pictures and/or words on poster board to visually represent ideas. And, it helps minimize students' self-consciousness by providing something to refer to while they talk about themselves or other subjects. Also, open-ended questionnaires are useful. They stimulate thinking and can generate a lot of discussion— a valuable tool with a quiet classroom.

Pairing students up with one another to discuss a topic or to conduct an interview provides opportunities for students to get acquainted and a venue to comfortably share. After they've completed their interview or discussion, have each student introduce their new acquaintance and/or summarize the highlights of their discussion with the rest of the class.

Small group discussions allow for more spirited interactions yet still provide ample opportunities for even the most reticent student to get involved. In smaller groups, students can cover key class concepts, learn about other students' attitudes and ideas, and foster the development of good interpersonal communication skills. This same format works well with study groups and can extend students' learning and relationship experiences outside of the classroom setting.

Finally, use competitive strategies. Pitting groups of students against one another in playful, innocuous ways adds intrigue and excitement to the learning process. Begin with an in-class assignment. Break students into groups based on some difference (gender, eye color, or side of town where they reside). Then have them participate in the assignment while competing with one another for the most efficient, thorough, or creative outcome. This good hearted competition will generate your students' enthusiasm and stimulate their zest for learning.

Communication is integral to classroom success. Whether it's expressed through self-presentation methods, course material, or the interactions that transpire between teachers and their students, it's important to be aware of the messages being sent and the approaches and tools that can make your classroom the best learning experience possible.

Andrea Peck is an instructor of Communications at Cuyahoga Community College, Cleveland, OH.

TOPIC VII:

Technology in the Classroom

by Tinnie A. Banks

The use of technology in the classroom is not new; only the hardware and software have been updated and enhanced. Reel-to-reel tapes were once used to listen to music, a movie projector was needed to view movies, music was played on vinyl records with a turntable, television was only available in black and white, soap operas and some television shows were heard on the radio. Similar to other technological advances, each of these technologies has been replaced with hardware and software which is more user friendly, easier to use, more widely available and affordable.

The traditional lecture is most effective with the auditory learner where the delivery of instruction is usually instructor-led with the student forced to listening passively. Visual and tactile learners learn best with more illustrations and hands-on exercises respectively. There are numerous pre-produced technologies available that are better suited and more effective in addressing the needs of all learning styles.

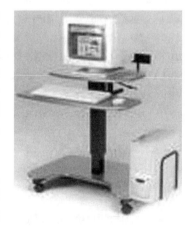

Technology in the classroom can be classified as hardware and software components: to present instruction or interactivity or to create units of instruction. A personal computer is an essential component on which software

Mobile personal computer unit

applications will be accessed and most peripheral equipment attached, i.e. projection unit, desktop video camera, SMART Board, DVD player, document camera. To easily view the contents of the monitor, a projection unit and large screen are used to enlarge the monitor's view and everything done which uses the computer. The projection unit can be an overhead projector attached to the LCD panel and the computer or a more expensive stand-alone projection unit. This equipment can be on a mobile cart to be shared with other instructors or stationary in the classroom. The college's audio-visual, media, or instructional television department is usually responsible for reserving and supporting the equipment.

Mobile unit with LCD projector

Desktop video conferencing and whiteboards are newer communications tools which provide the capability of interacting with other students or a guest speaker located at a remote site. To videoconference with another site, a desktop video camera, network connection and videocon-ferencing software similar to NetMeeting™ is required.

Once each of these items is correctly configured, videoconferencing can be done with a remote location. The instructor may join an existing videochat room or create one for the class to use and send e-mail to the participants.

Quickcam camera (top of monitor)

The whiteboard is similar to an old-fashioned blackboard but that works with multicolored dry erase markers instead of chalk. Words and illustrations can be written, captured, and

permanently recorded by either printing or creating an electronic version saved as a text file. The whiteboard also has an interactive touch screen to enhance training so the instructor can effectively demonstrate the steps involved in a linear operation. The whiteboard can also be used at a remote site where both sites can utilize the whiteboard and their respective input is visible to the remote site where ideas and results can be exchanged. The whiteboard

Smart whiteboard

is frequently available in the interactive video classroom but it can also be used at one location. In conjunction with a projection unit, the whiteboard can also serve as the projection screen.

The document camera has the capability of projecting all forms of media including x-rays, slides, transparencies, print media such as newspaper, artwork, maps and any object in three dimensions.

It has a zooming feature with an upper and lower lamp light. The document camera will usually be connected to the projection unit so that items can be enlarged for student viewing.

Textbooks are increasingly accompanied with complimentary interactive CD-ROMs which provide supplementary content and exercises. The instructor will need to review the contents of the CD-ROM to determine the appropriate time to introduce its material in

document camera

the curriculum. Homework assignments, supplementary con-

Interactive CD-ROM

tent, diagnostic tests using multimedia sound and graphics are usually included on the CD-ROMs. Exercises can be designed to give the student practice in discrimination, generalization, sequence, and psychomotor learning. Each is defined as follows:

    ❧   **Discrimination** is the ability to differentiate between several items,

- ❧ **Generalization** is the ability to put like items in groups,
- ❧ **Sequencing** teaches how to get things done in the right order, and
- ❧ **Psychomotor learning** teaches skills using the hands by simulating the physical activity.

Academic Systems uses interactive CD-ROMs to teach entire instructional units with engaging, interactive exercises and learning activities. It includes a web-based tool for assigning electronic homework that gives students immediate feedback on their work. Instructors also receive achievement reports that enable them to assess the students' progress. It enables students to work at their own pace and review instructions and explanations of the material with practice problems as needed.

Textbooks publishers are also including supporting web sites which provide supplementary instructional materials on the Internet for both the student and instructor. The instructional materials can include movies, interactive exercises, PowerPoint™ presentations and sometimes an electronic version of the textbook. In addition to World Wide Web addresses, the Internet can also be used to correspond with fellow classmates via e-mail. E-mail addresses and listservs are also being integrated into the curriculum by expanding interaction with the instructor and classmates outside of the normal class meeting time. A listserv is a group of users which may be students in the same class but can also include persons from anywhere in the world with a common interest that correspond with each other using an e-mail address. Messages posted to the listserv are distributed to all of its members. With the assistance of the information technology support staff at the college, the listserv can be created specifically for a course or the entire class can join an existing listserv owned and operated by professional journals and organizations such as the Media in Education and the Distance Education Forum.

There are other types of technology in the classroom that allow instructors to create multimedia instructional materials for presentation in the classroom. When designing multimedia instruction, one of the first steps should be determining the learning objectives for the presentation and one of the final steps should conclude by having the students perform some task integrating the information presented. The presentation software must be able to accommodate multiple forms of media, i.e., text, audio, video, graphics. PowerPoint, Hyperstudio™ and Astound™ software are commonly used in both business and educational settings. PowerPoint has an AutoContent Wizard which creates a presentation by requesting information from the presenter about the type of presentation (strategy, status), output options (presentation, Internet kiosk), presentation style (on-screen presentation, color or black & white overheads), and presentation options (title, author). Given this information, the wizard creates an editable presentation with a pre-selected background design and text which prompts the instructor for information to customize the slide show to meet their instructional goals.

Prior to integrating the desired media into the presentation, it must first become digitized or electronic. A scanner with a transparency adapter can digitize slides, overhead transparencies, x-rays, photographs and any object. The aforementioned

Quickcam desktop video camera can also take and create photographs and video clips. A digital camera takes and store photographs electronically either on a memory card or diskette, negating the need to scan the photographs. More advanced and expensive cameras also allow the creation of video clips. An advantage to using digital cameras is the ability to see the stored image after the photograph is taken. The pictures can then be accessed from the camera by connecting it to the personal computer and downloading the photographs from the camera. The instructor can store the files as picture or .jpeg graphic images, both can be integrated into presentation software that has both IBM-compatible and Macintosh versions. Once the majority of the media has been collected and digitized, it can be added with the text into the presentation.

The personal computer (both laptops and handhelds) is now the gateway to the use of technology in the classroom. Technology in the classroom was once disparate, stand-alone pieces of equipment designed to display a single form of media. The Internet, personal computers, peripheral equipment and corresponding software have given the instructor additional tools with the technological capability to engage all learners. In order to take advantage of these available technologies, the instructor will need to become both computer and Internet proficienct. Determine your existing skill level and gaps and design a personal training plan to achieve your desired level of technological literacy. Attend workshops, credit or non-credit course offerings. Preparing yourself to take advantage of the tools available in the new and improved technology classroom.

Tinnie A. Banks is Instructional Design Media Coordinator at Lorain County Community College, Elyria, OH.

TOPIC VIII:

What is Critical Thinking?

By Elizabeth T. Tice

What is Critical Thinking?

Actually, that is a good question. The word *thinking* can describe any number of cognitive activities and there is certainly more than one way to think. However, critical thinking has become a highly debated topic in educational circles in recent years. Elementary school teachers to graduate school professors are advocating that critical thinking be integrated into all curricula. But what is critical thinking anyway? Who defines it?

Critical thinking often refers to mental activity that typically originates in the left hemisphere of the brain. But is critical thinking more than being logical? It is true that critical thinking requires analytical and logical reasoning and demonstrates higher level thinking skills. But it is more than that. Understanding logic appears to be a necessary condition to become a critical thinker, however, it is not a sufficient condition. It is my belief that, while critical thinking requires logical reasoning skills, the two are not synonymous. Logic itself is not critical thinking.

In order for teachers to incorporate critical thinking into their classrooms, they must understand what it is and is not. Therefore, in this topic section we will examine some of the current definitions and debates around critical thinking and how critical thinking can be viewed in the construct of cognitive development theory. We will also explore the relationship between thinking logically and thinking critically and the effect of emotion on critical thinking.

Definitions of Critical Thinking

Ask ten people who believe themselves knowledgeable about critical thinking for a definition, and you will most likely receive ten differing responses. It seems that, although we have agreed upon the importance of critical thinking skills, we are struggling with the conceptual details.

Part of the problem may be that a dominant theoretical model of critical thinking does not yet exist. Definitions seem to vary by context (Tucker, 1996). As the Dean of the College of General Studies (and an instructor of critical thinking) at the University of Phoenix, I have endured many faculty debates on what we should actually teach in a Critical Thinking course.

Browne and Keeley (1986) refer to critical thinking as filtering—separating the relevant from the irrelevant. Chaffee (1985) says that critical thinking is "making sense of our world by carefully examining our thinking and the thinking of others in order to clarify and improve our understanding" (p. 49). Others (Missimer, 1990; Kahane, 1992; Beardsley, 1975; Freeman, 1993) define critical thinking much more technically: understanding argument, recognizing fallacies, distinguishing premises from conclusions, and isolating salient issues from irrelevant information.

Brookfield (1987) long considered an "expert" on critical thinking, contends that critical thinking is a process. Although his definition includes emotional as well as rational components, and clearly acknowledges the importance of culture and context, it contains the following common characteristics:

1. Identifying and challenging assumptions,
2. Challenging the importance of context,
3. Trying to imagine and explore alternatives, and
4. Reflective Skepticism (pp. 7-9).

Brookfield also defines reflective skepticism as the act of constantly questioning the status quo. Just because something has been believed for years does not necessarily mean that it is true. Just because someone of perceived importance (like professors, for example) says something is right, that does not prove that it is right. I like to call this the "maybe—maybe not" life stance.

To all the above definitions, I say—yes. They all describe, to one extent or another, critical thinking. Actually the above definitions have many things in common, although the terminology might differ. The common threads throughout most writers' beliefs are (a) the importance of a good foundation in formal and informal logic, (b) the willingness to ask questions, and (c) the ability to see the relevant answers, even if they don't coincide with our pre-existing beliefs.

Critical Thinking in the Construct
of Cognitive Development

It is helpful to examine critical thinking through the construct of cognitive development theory. Many cognitive theorists believe that concrete logic is not possible until at least age 6 or 7, and that only in the highest levels of cognitive development can critical thinking take place. Jean Piaget, a noted psychologist and developmental theorist, postulates the following stages of development:

1. **Sensimotor Stage**: Birth to age 2 (approximately). Children begin with no thinking structures (called schema) and develop them through exploration of their senses and experimentation on the environment. Significant cognitive development occurs, but children in the sensorimotor stage are incapable of logical thought.

2. **Pre-Operational Stage**: Ages 2 to 7 (approximately). Children rapidly develop language skills and more sophisticated cognitive structures but are still pre-logical. They are not capable of conservation (the ability to understand that substance does not change although it

changes shape or form). They are also incapable of de-centering (the ability to see things from another's perspective). Conservation and de-centering are prerequisite to logical thinking.

3. **Concrete Operational Stage**: Ages 7 to adolescence. Children begin to grasp conservation and de-centering. They begin to question: How does Santa really get to all those houses in one night? They can now reason logically but only on a concrete level, not hypothetically or abstractly. They solve problems logically but haphazardly.

4. **Formal Operations Stage**: Adolescence and above. The person is now capable of sophisticated logical thought. He or she can think in the abstract, can think hypothetically and can solve problems using the logic of combinations (Dworetzky & Davis, 1989).

Piaget's stages ended with Formal Operations, but Riegel (1973) has postulated a fifth stage called **Dialectical Reasoning**. This is a stage beyond logic where, I believe, real critical thinking lies. It is the ability to perceive the frequent paradoxes in life (to see the dialectic) and to question and analyze the assumptions that underlie the logic. Dialectical thinkers "readily recognize, accept, and even enjoy conflict and contradictions in values and possible courses of action because sorting out these conflicts forces them to grow intellectually" (Dworetzky & Davis, 1989, p. 360). A logical thinker can recognize and analyze the relationships between premises and conclusions. A critical thinker is able to extract and examine the assumptions that underlie the premises.

The Relationship between Logic and Critical Thinking

As stated earlier, logical reasoning seems to be a necessary, but not a sufficient condition for the development of critical thinking skills. It appears that one must be able to think logically, recognize fallacious reasoning, and construct valid arguments in order to think things through critically. However, one can understand the format of valid syllogisms, yet have no ability to understand cultural context or challenge assumptions. This seems to be at the core of most definitions of critical thinking. Skills in logical analysis provide the tools necessary to become a critical thinker.

In my Critical Thinking classes, I use the story of Jack and the Beanstalk to demonstrate the concept of challenging assumptions (an exercise shared with me by Toni LaMotta, a faculty colleague at the University of Phoenix). I ask students to relate the story and then ask them to name the hero of the story. Without hesitation, most of them name Jack. We then look at Jack's behavior in the story: he disobeyed his mother, he trespassed on the Giant's property, he stole the Giant's possessions, and he ultimately murdered the Giant. The compelling question here is—Who decided that Jack is a hero? The answer is that we did, culturally speaking. A critical thinker can see the underlying cultural assumptions in everyday happenings.

A critical thinker can understand that, although terrorism is abhorrent, it can be understood when viewed from the *cultural perspective* of the terrorist. A purely logical thinker will accept the following syllogism: Terrorism against the US is bad. The Islamic Jihad are terrorists against the US. Therefore the Islamic Jihad are bad. A critical thinker will not condone that act of terrorism, but will understand that there is more to the story than this simple, logically valid syllogism presents. He or she will understand that the Islamic Jihad are very similar to the early American revolutionaries; that they believe passionately in their cause; that in their culture this cause is all important; that the United States has manipulated their country for years, and that they could not possibly fight the United States on our terms. Saddam Hussein showed the world what happens to anyone who tries to fight the most powerful nation in the world in a conventional war. The early revolutionaries understood this and committed acts (such as the Boston Tea Party) that the British population living comfortably in England surely viewed as terrorism.

A critical thinker understands the cultural context of both examples and why Americans call the revolutionaries in our past *heroes*, yet call the Islamic revolutionaries *terrorists*.

Emotionality and Critical Thinking

From a purely logical perspective, any emotion is illogical. In fact, *appeal to emotion* is one of the most common logical fallacies. Seech (1993) writes extensively about logical vulnerability. He defines logical vulnerability as the inability to be logical about a given issue because one is too emotionally invested in it.

However, in the transition from logical thinking to critical thinking, emotion and intuition must be re-introduced to the equation. The difference, I believe, lies in the thinker's ability to recognize the impact of emotion on logical thinking, and to choose the best alternative that allows for the importance of both logic and intuition. A critical thinker can believe passionately in his or her own religious belief system, yet still maintain a big picture understanding that it is not the *only acceptable* religious belief system.

Brookfield (1987) asserts that the journey to critical thinking often begins with a highly emotional "trigger event" (p. 26). These events often have the effect of jolting us out of our comfort zones, forcing us to explore new territory. Trigger events can be positive or negative, although most anecdotal literature supports growth from negative events.

However, positive trigger events can also propel one down the road to critical thinking. Here is where we as educators can make a difference. Formal higher education often promotes critical thinking as does exposure to individuals whose critical thinking skills are more fully developed than our own (Brookfield, 1986). Typically, a trigger propels us into a period of appraisal. We internally explore the nature of the new learning. Many times a person becomes uncomfortable with the dissonance (a natural response) and tends to minimize and deny the new learning (Brookfield, 1986).

According to Brookfield (1986), the period of appraisal is followed by a period of exploration. Having finally accepted that the discrepancy and dissonance are real, we set out to make sense of it. We explore new ways to think and view the world. This exploration leads to the awareness of alternative perspectives and, paradoxically, the understanding that the abundance of alternatives often signals the lack of any one right choice. This phase is, in my opinion, the most difficult for people to endure.

Eventually, those who endure the anxiety come to Brookfield's final phase of Integration. Integration can involve radical life changes or invisible internal cognitive life changes. But change occurs.

Perhaps the reason that we have struggled so with a single definition of critical thinking is that it cannot be narrowly contained. Perhaps the fact that it seems to vary by context does not indicate that we have been inconsistent in our definition process; perhaps a core element of critical thinking is that it does indeed vary by context. And maybe we should just accept that. Not everything can be neatly categorized in our comfortably distinct boxes. After all, an important characteristic of critical thinkers is the ability to tolerate ambiguity and to discern among several shades of gray.

References

Beardsley, M. (1975). *Thinking straight*. Englewood Cliffs, NJ: Prentice-Hall.

Brookfield, S. (1986). *Developing critical thinkers.* San Francisco: Jossey-Bass.

Browne M. & Keeley, S. (1986). *Asking the right questions: A guide to critical thinking.* Englewood Cliffs NJ: Prentice-Hall.

Chaffee, J. (1985). *Thinking critically.* Boston: Houghton Mifflin Co.

Dworetzky, J. & Davis, N. (1989). *Human development: A lifespan approach.* New York: West Publishing Co.

Freeman, J. (1993). *Thinking logically.* Englewood Cliffs, NJ: Prentice-Hall.

Govier, T. (1988). *Selected issues in logic and communication.* Belmont, CA: Wadsworth.

Kahane, H. (1992). *Logic and contemporary rhetoric.* Belmont, CA: Wadsworth.

Missimer, C. (1990). *Good arguments: An introduction to critical thinking.* Englewood Cliffs, NJ: Prentice-Hall.

Riegel, K. (1973). Dialectical operations: The final period of cognitive development. *Human Development, (16),* 346-370.

Seech, Z. (1993) *Open minds and everyday reasoning.* Belmont, CA: Wadsworth.

Seymour, D. & Beardslee, E. (1990). *Critical thinking activities.* Palo Alto, CA: Seymour Publications.

Tucker, R. (1997). Less than critical thinking, Part I. *Adult Assessment Forum VI*(3), 3-6.

Dr. Elizabeth T. Tice is the Dean, College of General Studies; University of Phoenix, Tempe, AZ.

TOPIC IX:

The Syllabus and Lesson Plan

By Kay Stephan

The old cliché, "You never get a second chance to make a good first impression" is especially true for the syllabus. The syllabus can give students the impression that you are organized and know the subject matter as well as how to present it; or it can give the impression that you are disorganized and do not know how to run a class. Just as in other situations, the first impression may or may not be true; however, most would prefer making that first impression in a classroom a favorable one.

The syllabus provides your students with a roadmap of what the course will cover and what is expected of them. It will cover policies and provide information necessary for the successful completion of the course. In addition to providing directions, the syllabus should also be thought of as a contract between you and your students. Students know what they need to do to earn the desired grade, including readings, term papers, quizzes, tests, and other activities. A good syllabus will also provide policies such as "make-up" work and attendance. Take the advice of experienced teachers: the time and care taken to build a good syllabus will reap many benefits the entire term. The carefully written syllabus will protect you and your college when students try to alter the rules or challenge grades. If students see policies up front, there should be relatively few questions that can later cause problems. For instance if there is a request for a make-up exam, you should be able to refer to your syllabus and answer the question in a way that is fair to all students, not just the one requesting the make-up exam.

At first glance it could appear that this detailed syllabus is restrictive to your academic freedom. However, it's better to think of it as a guide and even a checklist that provides details of course requirements and college policies that could prevent misunderstandings and grievance procedures as well as providing students with a prescription for success. The outline that is described below can be thought of as a skeleton. An instructor is free to add information and put the syllabus in any format that is clear, readable, and reproducible.

In order to manage the numerous syllabus components, the syllabus will be split into three sections: the general course and instructor information, specific course requirements, and college policies.

General Course and Instructor Information

These components are basic, require little explanation, and are usually placed at the beginning of the syllabus. The parts are as follows:

- ❧ **Course Title**
- ❧ **Course Number**
- ❧ **Number of credit hours**
- ❧ **Class meeting days and times**
- ❧ **Term name and year**
- ❧ **Course description and prerequisites** (This information should be available in the college catalog; however, you may wish to expand it to better describe your specific course.)
- ❧ **Instructor's name and title**
- ❧ **Instructor's office telephone number**
- ❧ **Instructor's office hours**
- ❧ **Instructor's home phone number** (Optional)
- ❧ **Instructor's e-mail address**

Specific Course Requirements

These components explain specifically what the course is and what is expected of each student. This is the most crucial section and provides the most salient information. Any logical order of the components is acceptable.

- Be sure to list all **required materials**, including author(s), title, and edition of the textbook(s). You should also include all supplies, equipment and/or other special needs. It is difficult to require a student to purchase an expensive calculator in the middle of the semester, especially if the "drop class" period has passed. You need to determine all materials necessary, not covered by some type of course fee, that the student must purchase.

- One of the hardest things for many adjuncts to write is the **course rationale**. This explains how the course fits into the student's curriculum as well as why the course is of value in and of itself. You could ask a coordinator or department head about curriculum matters and if the course is a degree requirement. However, it is a good process for you, as the instructor, to think about the value or rationale for the course. This process can provide you with insight and direction for preparing your curriculum. (If you cannot verbalize the value of the course, then what do you think your students will find valuable about it?)

- A good syllabus will provide **course learning outcomes**. Your college may already have basic outcomes for each course in the curriculum. Again, check with your coordinator or department head to be sure that all minimum standards are met. Naturally, you may wish to add an outcome or two, but the basic ones should be consistent across all course sections. These outcomes should not be just words on a paper, but rather a guide that provides direction on what needs to be covered and mastered within the course. Since these outcomes are the backbone of your course, consider them carefully and determine how each will be measured.

- ❧ Some college administrations recommend **a statement about assessment**. Since most college instructors are now required to be very attentive to assessment activities, students should also know what assessment is, why it is important, what activities will be included in the course, and what, if any, activities will be considered a part of the grade. (In my class I have an ungraded pre-test, and the graded comprehensive final exam is considered the post-test. However, some instructors use a series of ungraded activities. Whatever you plan, students need to know how assessment activities will be used.)

- ❧ You need to carefully decide all the **course requirements** before preparing your syllabus. Since the syllabus is considered a contract, you cannot add requirements halfway through the term. The requirements may include quizzes, tests, papers, journalizing, readings, portfolios, etc. You could even include attendance as part of the requirements. Just be sure to include everything the students need to successfully complete the course.

- ❧ The syllabus should also include a **brief statement of the instructional methods** you will use. Examples of these include but are not limited to lecture, group work, films, guest speakers, panel discussions, and question-and-answer drills. Providing instructional methods will give students a preview of the class and what could be expected to happen during class sessions.

- ❧ Perhaps the most tedious task of preparing the syllabus is providing **a content outline for the entire course**; however, once designed, it will provide an excellent guide for daily class preparation for you as the instructor as well as for your students. This section should include a tentative outline of class topics and critical dates such as assignment due dates, tentative exam dates, holiday(s), and/or days when the class will not meet.

- ❧ At the heart of an good syllabus is **the section on grad-**

ing strategies and criteria. Students need to know how their final grade will be computed. For example, four tests may be worth 100 points each for a maximum of 400 points of the 1000 points possible, or the average of any number of tests may count as 40% of the grade. No matter how you set up your grading system, be sure to provide a grading scale and percentage weights of all components of the final grade. Include how the percentage grades will be converted into a letter grade, i.e. 94% earns an "A" while 93% earns an "A-." (If your school has a required grading scale, it would be in the college catalog.) Your grading criteria should include policies for accepting and/or evaluating assignments submitted after due dates, make-up test policies, etc. You may require that all work be turned in the day the student returns to class after an absence. It could be that quizzes cannot be made up and the lowest grade is dropped. You could also require a student to call you if they are going to miss a test. If the student does not follow the policy, then the test cannot be made up. Whatever you decide, be sure to express policies clearly on the syllabus and orally point them out during the first day of class. Not providing a concrete policy for make-up work can become a crux of controversy involving you, your students, and the administration.

෨ If you have an **attendance policy,** include it in your syllabus with clear instructions on how attendance counts in the final grade. Check the college catalog to see if there is a college-wide attendance policy. (An effective policy that I put in all my syllabi is that the student gets 10 bonus points for missing no more than one class for any reason.)

College Policies
This last section deals with policies that the college has developed for all students. This information is basically boilerplate and may

be available on disk. These policies may include the following:

- ❧ **Registration Policy** – This has to do with students on the college's official class lists and when students may no longer attend classes if their names do not appear on the list.
- ❧ **Students with Disabilities Policy**
- ❧ **Inclement Weather Policy**
- ❧ **Withdrawal Policy**
- ❧ **Fees and Refund Schedules**
- ❧ **Term Calendar** – This would list when classes begin, when the college is closed, final refund dates, last day to drop and add classes, and the final examination period.

Once you have completed your course syllabus, you are well on your way to planning an effective course. Some authorities feel that the syllabus is the most important document in academia since it defines the course and all requirements. Yes, it takes a great deal of time to design a good syllabus; but like most things involved with teaching, the first time is the most difficult. After all, you can make minor adjustments as necessary to refine the original syllabus. Also, once you have major policies worked out, many can be transferred from course to course. Take the time necessary to plan your syllabus. It will be worth it and will certainly make that first impression a good one.

The Lesson Plan

The lesson plan is a "must do" for effective teaching. If you have a well-designed course outline, the daily lesson plan is much easier to prepare. These are numerous formats for lesson plans; you need to select one that works for you. (Some teachers use a loose-leaf notebook to keep lesson plans and notes; others use one file folder for each lesson and even color codes for different classes.) While the syllabus is fairly cut and dry, the lesson plan can reflect your creative side. It can reflect your personality and teaching style as long as it directs effective learning.

Before you start to plan the lesson, you need to determine the day's objectives. These are the focal point of any plan. You must know what you need to teach, and you must be able to verbalize it to your students. There can be a variety of ways of attaining the objectives, but you first need to decide what they are.

After determining your objectives, then outline the major topics you will cover, including definitions and reference to sources that are not included in the textbook. With computer slide presentations available with many textbooks, the chapter outlines may already be prepared. (I print the outlines and then add my supplementary notes. For long or difficult concepts, I may even print the outline for students. Doing this allows them to focus on the lesson instead of taking copious notes.)

Next you will need to determine how you will get the major points across to students. Lecturing, of course, is one way; but it may not always be the most effective strategy. This is where your creativity and imagination come into play. Adding personal anecdotes and experiences help bring a lesson to life. You should also try to stimulate active student participation. Generally students will retain knowledge much longer if they actively participate in the classroom activity.

Any experienced teacher can recall classroom episodes where things did not go as planned. Equipment didn't work, an activity fell flat, or students did not understand the lecture. That is why the best lesson plan allows for flexibility, and the best teachers can adjust to unpredictable experiences and audiences. But no matter what happens, if the lesson objectives are identified, the teacher can adjust his or her teaching approach and still meet the objectives.

Your lesson plan should include everything you need to take to the classroom such as notes, handouts, or computer disks. It should also include instructor and student activities and homework assignments with due dates.

(In many of my classes I have adopted the practice of preparing a weekly agenda for each student. The agenda includes daily objectives, what chapters will be covered, and the homework assignments with due dates. Students appreciate having this written documentation in order to plan their busy week in advance. I also have a file folder in the classroom where student know they can pick up the agenda if they have missed a class.)

Planning is the job of all good teachers. Whether it is the syllabus or the daily lesson plan, you must spend the time necessary to plan effective learning strategies. You should also make notes on the lesson plans to remind yourself of what activities worked well and which ones need to be modified. Keeping a careful record of your lessons will make teaching easier from year to year. You will also develop a portfolio of ideas and activities that you can use in many teaching situations. Take the time and plan!

Kay Stephan is the Director of Adjunct Faculty, University of Akron, Wayne College, Orrville, OH.

TOPIC X:

Motivating the Student in the College Classroom

By Hikmat Chedid

Delivering a well-prepared lecture is just one of the necessary conditions for achieving success in today's classrooms. A successful instructor realizes that achieving success requires ensuring that students, and specifically the less attentive students, are motivated to comprehend and retain the material. The literature clearly reflects that motivation is essential to achieving excellence in the classroom. The following are methods I use in my classroom to engage the less motivated.

> ❧ **Deliver the first couple of lectures from the back of the classroom.**
> I began to notice over the years that less motivated students fill the seats that are farthest away from the instructor's desk. Those students, whom I get to know better later in the semester, tend to be less motivated but sometimes only shy and want to keep to themselves. I deliver my first lecture and some subsequent lectures from the back of the room, making clear but not aggressive eye contact with the students. These are attempts to confirm to them that they are important to me, and that they deserve and will be accorded personal attention. I think of it as a personal invitation to each of them to become an active participant in the classroom. Often students accept this invitation, and it turns out to be all that is required to

motivate a particular student to become active and to take ownership of his learning.

> **Assign extra credit points for class participation.**
> I assure students that I will not call on them to answer questions unless they indicate their willingness to answer the question by raising their hands. I however assign a healthy number of extra credit points toward class participation, and remind students often of their many predecessors who achieved a higher grade as a result of those extra credit points. I am always surprised to find that those points motivate even the most shy of students and convince him or her to participate regularly in classroom discussions. However it is imperative to compliment students on the quality of their questions: "Good question, Mr. Reeves, I am glad you asked about that..." "Excellent answer! Ms. Johnson..."

> **Ask students to express their goals for the course, and relate the course material to those goals.**
> I ask each student to introduce himself or herself during the first class, and to explain his or her reason for taking the course. From the students' comments, I synthesize several class goals. Subsequently, I begin my lectures by explaining how the material being presented relates to the long-term goals of the students. It is critical to explain to students, preferably through real examples, why they are learning a particular concept and how they will encounter the concept on the job.

> **Be enthusiastic about the subject matter, and show your enthusiasm.**
> Enthusiasm is contagious; an enthusiastic teacher thinks of unusual real-life examples to relate the concept. I let not only my body language—teaching on my feet, using good eye contact, standing close to the students, using a lively tone of voice (although sometimes I run the real risk of loosing my voice),

and radiating a positive overall demeanor—demonstrate a professional image and show my enthusiasm, but I truly have fun with the subject. I find myself acting out concepts, confronting common misconceptions, and presenting intuitive results. Have genuine fun in the classroom.

≈ **Have high but compassionate standards.**
High and positive expectations usually produce excellent and positive outcomes. Let me define the two terms. Most know what is meant by the term "high standard". If you guessed that it meant difficult exams and homework assignments that require a great time commitment, you are correct. "Compassionate" refers to a realization on the professor's part that some college students are not the traditional full-time "just out of high school" students. These students might be single parents or individuals holding two jobs. While the course outcomes must not be reduced to allow students to pass undeservedly, the professor must be willing to extend the student extra help on an one-on-one basis, and at times and hours that might not be ideal. I find that if students realize the applicability of an otherwise long and difficult project to their objective, and if they know their professor is genuinely willing to help them, they will rise to the occasion and become motivated to achieving success.

≈ **Provide a class structure that allows students to make mistakes, learn from their mistakes, and try again with little or no punitive measures.**
I allow students a chance to re-do and re-submit their exams for a higher grade. Not necessarily a full grade, but certainly an improved grade. I also explain to them that the same concept will appear on subsequent quizzes and examinations, particularly on the final exam. Those who learn from their current mistakes will avoid making them on a future quiz and as a result will earn higher grades. This method motivates students to research questions they missed, learn from their mistakes, and achieve better

mastery of the course concepts.

🙠 **Administer quizzes frequently, to motivate students to do assignments regularly.**

I ask students toward the beginning of the course to take a positive outlook on quizzes, and think of them as previews for the larger, more important examination. I encourage students to think of quizzes as a service to help them monitor their progress. Weekly quizzes motivate the student to do assignments regularly, uncover their problem areas, and make attempts to understand the concepts before the class is too far along. It is often required that the instructor hold one-on-one conferences with students who perform poorly on more than one quiz, but make no obvious attempt to improve.

🙠 **Create group activities to provide immediate experience with the concepts.**

Performance-based group activities reinforce and lend clarity to difficult concepts. Students often do not realize that they do not understand a certain concept until they attempt to apply the concept to case studies or to formulate a solution to a real problem. Group performance-based activities uncover those deficiencies, and provide students an opportunity to measure their learning. Often these group activities are the first opportunity a student has to learn to work successfully with a difficult person, to learn attributes that lead to a successful team dynamic, and to become a successful team member. When conflicts occur between team members, as tempting as it is to step in and resolve the matter, I refrain from doing so to avoid robbing students of the opportunity to resolve the problem on their own, and to feel proud as a result of their experience.

🙠 **Test fairly.**

Unfair examinations can discourage the best of students. However testing fairly does not mean giving easy exams. To the contrary, one can give difficult but fair examinations. By exam time, students should be clear on the test objectives. The exam should be limited to what are in those objectives. Difficult questions are encouraged as long as they are carefully examined after the exam is graded. Those questions missed by the majority of the students, should be factored out of the grade, evaluated for value added, explained to the class, and re-addressed in future quizzes and exams.

Achieving success in the classroom is directly correlated with the level of student motivation. Student motivation is a deliberate series of actions that can and should be designed into the course by the professor. One might correctly argue that certain students come to the classroom with excellent motivation and do not require additional effort by the instructor. However, motivating those students who lack that motivation is where the challenges and the rewards exist.

Hikmat Chedid is Assistant Professor of Engineering at Lorain County Community College, Elyria, OH.

TOPIC XI:

Collaborative/Cooperative Learning

By Arlene Sego

Collaborative learning (also called cooperative learning) is one of the oldest educational techniques, dating back to one-room schoolhouses where several grades were grouped together. In theory, collaborative learning brings students of differing abilities together in small groups where they teach each other the concepts of the formal class by reinforcing lecture and text materials. In practice, student groups either work on assigned projects cooperatively or take selected quizzes and/or tests together. The process forced all students to become actively involved in classroom activities. Even passive students are more inclined to become active when their participation is required for the ultimate success of their partners. Adult learners relate to collaboration in the classroom because of the similarity to the cooperation required in most contemporary workplaces.

College classrooms tend to have a more heterogeneous student base than those found in lower grades. But there are subtle differences between types of classes. Students in technical education classes are highly motivated, regardless of the specific academic skills they possess. Students in developmental classes generally will be hampered by the fact that they have fewer basic English and mathematics skills with which to solve problems. Traditional academic classes, however, will be a composite of students' abilities, purpose, and motivation. But no matter the type of class or teaching method, virtually all academic and technical disciplines can benefit from the inclusion of collaborative techniques in the classroom.

For instructors there are two basic prerequisites for collaborative learning: thorough planning and a *total* commitment. As a facilitator, the instructor becomes an idea person, a resource person, a mediator (conflict resolution is as much of an accomplishment in collaborative education as it is in the workplace or in life itself), and a supporter of the students' efforts.

Preliminary planning by faculty for collaborative classroom activities includes the determination of classroom goals, specific activities that can be assigned cooperatively, and the balance sought with traditional teaching methods. Ideally a collaborative activity should be started the first week of class. If grades are going to be assigned for group work, the students must be made aware of this at the beginning of the term; the assignment of the same grade to each member of a group is the incentive needed to make collaboration work effectively. Adult learners always are concerned about how they will be graded in a class, so students should be informed what part of the final grade will be the result of the collaborative efforts.

The optimum size for a work group is four or five students, especially if the students are working on a project or other activity that will be graded. More than five students can be unwieldy while fewer than four opens the door to domineering students. Groups can be formed by:

- students themselves,
- the instructor assigning students to groups,
- random assignment, or
- selection based upon similar interests or specific criteria.

However, decided disadvantages accompany student-based selection. Students often choose to be with friends (which excludes assimilation of new students into the mainstream of the class) and there may be stress in arranging groups if students do not know each other and have no basis for selection.

Some collaborative experiences will lend themselves to completion during one class period while others will take days or even weeks to complete. Overlapping activities will add to the cohesiveness of the group structure. Giving students the opportunity to talk with each other begins the interaction that is one of the important components for success in collaborative learning.

Not all collaborative activities need to be structured or grade-based. Students will respond to a change in classroom pace when they have the opportunity to react with partners. Group work can be used to reaffirm techniques that have been presented, analyze material from differing perspectives, or brainstorm for solutions to problems presented by the instructor. Let students know what is expected from them during their impromptu activity so it does not become a social event.

Although it is important to give explicit instructions about the nature and purpose of a collaborative activity plus how groups are to operate, leave students latitude for their own group innovations. The instructor is the facilitator for activities. Students are the active participants. Provide a classroom atmosphere whereby students feel free to contribute creative ideas without fear of criticism.

When students are able to physically move chairs together for group activities they can focus on each other, rather than the teacher. If a classroom has tables and chairs or desks permanently attached to the floor, allow students to move so that they are in close proximity to each other. Groups inherently try to physically move away from other groups of students. Interestingly, collaboration invariably brings a louder than usual level and excitement to the classrooms, but students are so engrossed helping each other they tend to ignore the other groups.

Adults can be sensitive to how others view them and tend to be more candid when working in small groups; working with fellow students provides adults the opportunity to explore new horizons in their subject area.

The benefits of collaborative learning include:

- ❧ Adults have a vehicle **to get to know others** in class,
- ❧ **Attendance tends to be better** (a result of a commitment to the group),
- ❧ **Improved grades** due to increased understanding of the subject matter,
- ❧ Classroom groups **foster study groups** outside of the class, and
- ❧ Students **become active participants** in their own learning.

Teachers regularly must re-evaluate their classroom styles to accommodate changes in technology, student abilities, and student demands. Collaborative learning is but one of many viable strategies to encourage participation by students. Obstacles that might be encountered are: some students may feel they paid money to take the course, therefore the teacher should stand in front of the class and lecture; groups may not take an assignment seriously; and some individuals may have difficulty working within a group. However, problems can be overcome by involving students in decisions regarding the progression of collaborative activities.

Many colleges now provide students with the opportunity to achieve educational goals outside the traditional classroom setting by the use of "distance learning" (courses taught via the Internet, telecourse instruction, or instruction by compressed video). At first glance there is a perception that students will only learn facts, without the opportunity to develop critical thinking skills. But interaction between students and with the faculty member can be achieved through the use of e-mail, bulletin boards, or chat rooms. More progressive institutions of higher learning already provide campus e-mail for students and faculty, so it is worthwhile to find out what is available for adjunct faculty and part-time students.

No one method of teaching can ever be an end unto itself. The use of collaborative learning is but one of many viable classroom strategies to encourage the participation of your students. But with its use adult students tend to be more comfortable in an academic setting, which translates into improved subject matter skills and the desire to continue their education.

Arlene Sego *has served as adjunct faculty mentor/trainer and is the author of several publications on cooperative/collaborative learning, Williamsburg, VA.*

TOPIC XII:

Student Learning Styles: Teaching Techniques for the 21st Century

By Michael Parsons

Introduction: New Learning Paradigm

For the past decade a number of educational researchers have examined the characteristics of student learning. Previously it was assumed that students learned effectively by reading textbooks, listening carefully to synthesizing lectures, and applying deductive logic to examinations. Such well-known education researchers as Will McKeachie (University of Michigan), Howard Gardner (Harvard), and Pat Cross (University of California-Berkeley) now document that students learn best when they are involved directly with the materials they are to learn.

A number of new strategies are being advanced to improve student ownership of learning. Focused discussion has become a popular model at a number of colleges and universities. Cooperative learning uses teams of students to address problem solving and application skills. Twenty-first century technology including CD-ROMs, interactive television, and the Internet provide the students with both input and control over the material being learned. All of these techniques require varying degrees of access to technology or the commitment of large blocks of instructional time.

While effective, they tend to lack both spontaneity and efficiency. There is a design for instruction that is as effective as those aforementioned, supports spontaneity, and can be tailored effectively to fit a variety of time and teaching frames.

The Nominal Group Technique

In 1968 two social psychologists, AndreL. Debecq and Andrew VandeVen designed a strategy called the Nominal Group Technique (NGT). It can be used to turn a heterogeneous class into a structured group for decision making. It may be applied in a variety of classes. Data provided by the instructor allows the students to engage in analysis, synthesis, and evaluation activities. These higher order thinking skills enhance student knowledge and put the student in control of his or her learning. The process has four steps:

1. **The data is provided to the students**. Each student is then asked to react individually by comparing his or her attitude, value, or demographic base to the general summary.

2. **A round-robin discussion** then allows all members of the class to react to diverse responses.

3. **A summary of class responses** is prepared which then becomes a micro-dataset to be compared with the larger one that initiated the activity.

4. **An analysis of the differences** between the class information and the larger dataset and **an evaluation of the potential causes** for any disparity complete the activity.

The foregoing description is somewhat abstract; let's consider each component of the activity to better understand how this technique can be applied in a variety of classroom settings.

Sources of Data

The NGT technique is particularly effective in social and behavioral science courses. A variety of federal and state organizations provide useful data summaries. I have used taxonomies of values derived from U.S. Department of Labor studies, prestige rankings of professions released by the U.S. Department of Interior, rankings of priorities for educational reform by U.S. Department of Education researchers, and rankings of student behavior drawn from studies produced by the American Council on Education. The information is available on the Internet, in daily newspapers (especially *USA Today*), and in weekly news magazines like *Time* and *U.S. News and World Report*. In each instance, individual student rankings and their class averages differed form the national databases. Student reactions to the strategy indicate that they are very interested in how they compare to other groups in society and are very willing to both analyze and evaluate the nature and causes of the divergence.

NGT Organizational Design

The following steps can be used to implement an NGT activity:

1. **Present a set of data to the students, preferably in writing**. Explain to them that they are to read the questions or statements, disregard the ranking provided with the data, and list their personal responses.

2. **The size of the dataset will determine the amount of time given to individual ranking**. I endeavor to use datasets that do not exceed two dozen questions or responses. The amount of time it takes for individual responses usually does not exceed 7-10 minutes.

3. Once the students are finished with individual rankings, **a general discussion is held of the types of responses elicited from the class**. The purpose of the round-robin is to enhance the student feeling of participation and ownership of the material.

4. Following the discussion, **students and the instructor construct a class response summary**. If the dataset is long, the instructor may choose to prepare the summary outside of class.

5. Using the summary as a guide, the instructor fa-
    cilitates **an analysis of the similarities and dif-
    ferences between the class summary and the
    dataset**. Students expand their personal owner-
    ship as well as begin the process of the class be-
    coming a group in the sociological sense.

6. The final step in the process is a synthesis. The
    students, guided by the faculty member, **evalu-
    ate the degree of congruence between course
    theory and the real world application** reflected
    throughout the dataset.

This activity adds a dimension of reality to course theory as
well as assisting students in understanding how their classroom
learning can be applied in the real world. Comments like "this
is the first time I have ever understood what to do with course
material" are not uncommon.

Questions Frequently Asked About NGT

❧ **How many people can participate?**
In general, nominal groups are best with membership of
approximately 8 to 10. It is relatively easy to divide a class
of 30 into three of these groups. The faculty member as
facilitator can move comfortably from one to another
during the process of constructing a class response
summary. Also, discussion can be class wide or in subsets.
The strategy had a great deal of flexibility, depending
upon classroom climate and instructor flexibility.

❧ **What characterizes a good dataset?**
Research into student learning styles reports that students
bring with them attitudes, feelings, and mental models
that impact on teaching/learning. Any dataset that allows
students to compare their generic perceptions with those
that are attitude- or values-based and short enough that
they do not require class periods for application and
analysis.

ꝏ **What skills are required of students to use the technique?**

In general, it is best to not use a technique like NGT until the class has begun to develop a sense of identity. The process is effective to the extent that the students are willing to share with each other and communicate relatively openly about values- and attitudes-based material. In general, I do not use these techniques until approximately one month into the semester or term. If a class is reticent to participate verbally, I would recommend simpler skill-building initiatives prior to using something as complex as NGT.

ꝏ **What skills should the faculty member/facilitator possess?**

The facilitator must have a comfort level with a variety of communication skills but most specifically listening and synthesizing. During both the discussion phase and summary-building phase, the facilitator must hear what the students are saying and, if uncertain, synthesize the responses as a way of seeking agreement. Also, the individual must have established a rapport with the class so that the students are willing to share and discuss emotionally charged material. Finally, the facilitator must be able to articulate the purpose of the exercise within the context of the purpose of the course. If the students do not feel "connected," their participation will be superficial.

ꝏ **Are there disadvantages to NGT? When shouldn't it be used?**

NGT is designed to foster higher order thinking, problem solving, and evaluation. It requires careful planning and a focused application. If the goal of the course is to simply encourage student presentation of material or student-to-student discussion, there are other less complex strategies that should be used.

Conclusion: Why do it?

Twenty-first century students expect more of their education. We need to support them as they develop critical-thinking skills, problem-solving strategies, and risk taking. Further, both students and employers are critical of education for not making students "work ready." NGT addresses all of these skills. If we are to be successful in preparing our clients for a rapidly changing world, we must "rethink our way."

Dr. Michael Parsons is the Dean of Instruction at Hagerstown Community College, Hagerstown, MD.

TOPIC XIII:

Teaching Students to Solve Problems

By Sheri Bidwell

One important way that instructors can prepare students for success in the workplace is to give them opportunities to learn and practice problem-solving skills. Problem solving has been identified as one of several critical workplace skills.

These and other skills, which were identified by the U.S. Secretary of Labor's Commission on Achieving Necessary Skills (SCANS), are listed below. The skills were identified and verified by a broad range of employers representative of business, industry, labor, and community-based organizations.

Foundation Skills: Effective workers need the following skills and qualities for solid job performance—
- **basic skills** (reading, writing, math, speaking, and listening);
- **thinking skills** (thinking creatively, decision making, problem solving, and knowing how to learn); and
- **personal qualities** (individual responsibility, self-esteem, sociability, self-management, and integrity).

Workplace Competencies: Effective workers need to productively use—
- **resources** (e.g., allocate time, money, materials, space, and staff);
- **interpersonal skills** (e.g., work in teams, teach others, serve customers, lead, negotiate, and work well with people from culturally diverse backgrounds);
- **information** (e.g., acquire and evaluate data, organize and maintain files, interpret and communicate, and use computers to process information);
- **systems** (e.g., understand social, organizational, and technological systems; monitor and correct performance; design or improve systems); and
- **technology** (e.g., select equipment and tools, apply technology to specific tasks, maintain and troubleshoot equipment).

Teaching students problem-solving skills is important for several reasons, including:

- ❧ It **gives students practice at solving problems** that resemble those found in the workplace.

- ❧ It **helps students learn a process** that can be applied to many different problems.

- ❧ **Problem-solving activities can support all of the SCANS skills.**

- ❧ When done with others (in pairs or teams of three to five students), **problem-solving activities help students develop and practice other SCANS skills** (e.g., teamwork, effective communication [being clear, listening, negotiating], responsibility, self-esteem).

By now, you may be saying to yourself, "I already have too much to cover. Now you're telling me to teach more?" The good news is that teaching problem-solving skills doesn't have to be a topic that is singled out and taught in isolation. Instead, it is an instructional strategy that can be used to teach in any subject area. It is recommended that you teach the basics of problem solving first, and then give students opportunities to solve problems related to your course content.

Experienced instructors recommend these steps:

1. **Begin to teach students the basics of problem solving by helping them realize that there is a** *process* **that they already use when encountering everyday problems.** Such problems might include fixing a paper jam in a photocopy machine, selecting a long-distance carrier, or repairing equipment. So ask them about their everyday problems. Ask questions that require students to describe in detail the steps they take when solving those problems.

2. **Help students isolate the steps involved in the problem-solving process.** If you wish, share the steps described in the IDEAL problem-solving model. It was designed as an aid for teaching and improving prob-

lem-solving skills. The IDEAL process includes the following steps:

I = **Identify the problem** (i.e., determine what needs to be done).

D = **Define the problem** (i.e., sharpen and clarify the boundaries).

E = **Explore alternative approaches** (i.e., gather information to determine the available options, analyze and evaluate alternatives, and choose the best one, taking into account many variables, including cost, time, human resources, materials, environment, and expertise).

A = **Act on a plan** (i.e., determine the logical steps to be used and how to progress through the steps).

L = **Look at the result** (i.e., determine whether or not the plan worked).

3. **Develop or choose learning activities that give students opportunities to develop and/or refine their problem-solving skills.** These activities can be related to or separate from the subject area. The options for developing activities that promote problem solving are nearly endless!

The following guidelines may be helpful:

~ **Allow the students to be at the center of their own learning**. After all, people don't learn how to solve problems by being told the correct solution—they learn by doing.

~ **Assign open-ended tasks** (instead of those with one right answer). For example, an assignment to select an effective marketing campaign to meet a given set of criteria is open-ended. So is an assignment to design and build a product that addresses a need.

- **Minimize instructions** so that students are encouraged to invent innovative ways to accomplish their tasks.

- **Provide students with a variety of materials** from which to choose (when appropriate).

- When students have questions, the best response is to **repeat the beginning instructions, without giving further information**. This strategy encourages students to work with teammates to figure out how to reach their goal.

- **Allow plenty of time for students to explore**. As long as students are actively engaged, learning is taking place.

- **Encourage students to share ideas with each other**. This strategy reflects how people solve problems in the workplace—with input from others. Most problem-solving activities lend themselves to having students work individually or in pairs. Occasionally, it is appropriate for students to work in teams of three to five. When students work individually, they should be encouraged to seek others' input. In addition, when problem-solving activities involve the manipulation of materials and equipment, it is important to assign students to work in both same-gender and mixed-gender groups.

Here's an activity that can be used to teach the basics of the problem-solving process:

Design and Build the Highest Tower

Challenge students to build the highest tower they can by using nontraditional materials. For each pair of students, provide two pieces of 8 °" x 11" paper, 10 paper clips, and a pair of scissors. To measure and compare the height of towers, you can use a yardstick or measuring tape.

1. **Instructions for Students:** Give students the following instructions (and no other information):

    Only the materials provided may be used to build the tower.

    The towers must be free standing; they may not lean against a wall or be held up.

    Towers must be brought to the tape on the wall for measuring (optional).

2. **Measurement:** Measure the height of each structure as it is finished. When all towers have been measured, announce the winners.

3. **Discussion:** Have students examine all of the towers. Encourage them to discuss the strategies that made some towers more successful than others. Ask students to describe the problem-solving process they used in designing and building their towers. Write a summary of the process for the whole class to see and agree on.

4. **Continuation:** Allow time for experimentation by instructing each team to build a second tower. This time, give them 15 minutes to experiment with scratch paper before they actually begin their second construction.

Related Activities: Have students do one or more of the following activities:

- Have students follow the parameters of a project budget. Develop a cost reporting sheet and assign monetary values to each material. For example:
- Give each team a budget of $1500. Tell them that the winning team will have the highest tower **and** come in under-budget. In case of a tie, the lowest-cost tower will win.
- Assign values to the materials: paper, $500; paper clip, $100; labor, $10/hour; technical assistance from the instructor, $100/minute.
- Write and present a sales presentation about the tower.
- Describe in writing the problem-solving process used throughout the design project. Include diagrams of the steps taken (if appropriate).

Variation: If students need more practice at using the problem-solving process, have student pairs use only newspaper, and no other materials or equipment, to construct the longest possible freestanding bridge.

Sheri Bidwell is a Consultant with Connections for Learning, Columbus, OH.

TOPIC XIV:

Large Class Teaching Tips

The following are short summaries of successful large class teaching methods used by the faculty at Iowa State University (ISU):

- **Create working teams in class.**
  Teams of six students are mixed randomly to play off each other's strengths. They discuss lecture materials in class and learn to be responsible for each other because individual quiz scores reflect the average performance of team members.

- **Create a non-threatening environment.**
  Bill Boon, landscape architect, plays music as students enter class and also includes a silly segment in each of his lectures to help remove barriers. "I think any subject can be made fun. I couldn't do it with algebra because I'm not in love with algebra," he said. "Our job as teachers is more to light candles than to fill vessels."

- **Be accessible.**
  Show up for class early and hang around after class so students can approach you individually. Some faculty provide their e-mail addresses to students and encourage them to send inquiries that way. They noted, though, that e-mail correspondence allows students to remain nearly anonymous.

- **Mix up the media used in the classroom.**
  Variety is important to keep students engaged and also to respond to different kinds of learning styles (visual vs. straight lecture vs. hands-on opportunities, for example.) Many use combinations of video clips,

35 mm slides, overhead sheets and demonstrations involving students in their classes.

❧ Use the technology.
One professor said he is a strong proponent of the use of PowerPoint™ software to present diagrams, key questions and photographs. Some said they are cautious about getting too caught up in the technology and losing track of students. A Ph.D. candidate said that as a student, she is frustrated by lectures that rely on PowerPoint. "It's colorful and pretty, but I can't put that pretty stuff in my notes."

❧ Assign creative projects.
Whether used as extra credit opportunities, key components in the course or an option to the final exam, some faculty believe student projects help personalize the class, particularly when the process requires students to submit proposals or receive feedback periodically from the instructor.

❧ Place "Help" boxes in the back of the classroom.
Students anonymously ask questions related to the course. One instructor prepares responses outside of class and answers questions at the beginning of each lecture.

❧ Ask "lecture challenge questions."
Presented to students near the end of class, the questions relate to a topic just covered, one soon to be covered or something related generally to the class. One professor said students' written answers provide her with a barometer of whether what she thinks she said is what they learned, student prejudices about a topic coming up, or insight into how to approach a puzzling or difficult topic.

❧ Pair students to help both learn better.
One of several "contract" options students may select for the course, this teams a strong student with a struggling student. It requires a time commitment, but

both in the pair typically perform better in class.

൙ **Develop a course homepage on the World Wide Web.**

A web page can reinforce or enhance the content of lecture classes. Steve Richardson's course page includes "Ask a geologist," an electronic version of the "Help" box; vocabulary lists; tutorials; sample test questions; and links to other web sites.

Printed with Permission—Inside Iowa State, *Iowa State University, Ames, IA.*

TOPIC XV:

Diversity in the Classroom

By Andrea Peck

At most institutions of higher learning, the student population is diverse. Whether it's a result of age, ethnic, life, work, or learning style differences, it's valuable to recognize these differences and their impact on your classroom.

Consider your students' ages when determining course content, the presentation of that content, and as a variable for better understanding their attitudes and behavior. For instance, when thinking of topics for a classroom discussion, use time frames, experiences and names that students would be familiar with. While older students may relate to information that enables them to reminisce about the past, as well as enjoy learning about the present, younger students may prefer topics that directly impact them now.

In understanding students attitudes and behaviors, keep in mind that many older students were raised in structured classroom settings. As a result, they're accustomed to formal lecture and discussion formats. Their younger counterparts, the MTV generation, have had more external stimulation and will probably respond to an active, entertaining learning approach. Thus, incorporate a variety of activities and visual aids to liven up your classroom and to appeal to a plethora of student interests and tastes.

Older students bring a variety of qualities—extensive life and work experiences and a clear focus and determination—to the classroom. Because most are attending college for the first time or returning to upgrade job positions and skills, they value their education. As a result, they're more likely than younger students to participate in the class. Capitalize on their desires to be vocal and to take initiative. Provide a forum for their feedback and interactions. And though younger students may be more familiar with course curricula, they may be less confident about their educational goals. Consequently, you may need to encourage them to be more active classroom participants.

Age also impacts behavior. Recently an older colleague complained about his younger male students wearing baseball caps in the classroom. In his day it was disrespectful for men not to remove their hats. As a result, he was misinterpreting his students' desire to be fashionable with past standards of appropriateness. So be aware. A variety of clothing and hair styles, as well as body ornaments, are not only appropriate but status quo in today's classroom.

Like age, gender and ethnic differences affect the classroom. Avoid topics that are sexually explicit, overly personal, or racially biased. Approach your students' learning with respect by refraining from generalizing, criticizing or praising anyone in particular and by treating all students fairly. Most of all, be sensitive. Some words and expressions may put a barrier between you and your students. Even something as seemingly harmless as gender descriptive language (i.e. salesman versus sales person) may put some students off.

Students come with a wide range of expectations for you and your classroom. Some will expect you to be counselors and assist them with both their academic and personal needs. Others need to be deprogrammed from negative attitudes that have accumulated from years of bad learning experiences. Some need a coach to encourage them along the way, while others will want you to show then how to practically apply their learning.

In addition to social, personal, and genetic differences, students have different learning styles. Extroverted learners learn best by interacting. These students like to express and exchange ideas because it enables them to sort through and understand them better. They'll benefit from open discussions and opportunities to interact with you and others right away.

Introverted learners need time to process ideas and concepts. They learn best by writing information down and then reviewing it later before they address you with any questions. These students work well independently, even within a group, on projects, or on class assignments.

The literal learner responds best to hands-on learning experiences that enable him or her to know something by actually doing it. Math, science and technology can be good subject areas for these students. They benefit from role playing and experiential learning as well.

Abstract learners respond best to creative assignments that allow them to discover and explore new and different perspectives on their topic. They like to learn and theorize about ideas through analogy, comparison, and metaphor. Writing, group discussions, and debates as well as a variety of artistic endeavors support their learning styles.

Some students are driven by accomplishment and will take on greater amounts of work the more they are expected to do. Extra credit and/or extra work requirements for higher grades motivate them. These students prefer to complete assignments prior to moving onto something new and having ample time to complete their work when or before it's due.

Finally, there are those students who like to work on a myriad of projects simultaneously. They have a tendency to get scattered, so keep them on task to ensure work completion. Their optimal performance will come as a result of having several assignments due as opposed to one or two major projects. They perform well under last minute time pressures.

Anymore, the classroom is comprised of heterogeneous audiences who not only learn in different ways, but who respond to and benefit from a variety of teaching approaches. As a result, instructors need to approach learning as diversely as the students who sit before them.

Andrea Peck is an instructor of Communications at Cuyahoga Community College, Cleveland, OH.

TOPIC XVI:

Preparing for a Distance Education Assignment

By Tinnie A. Banks

By definition, a distance education course will be delivered using telecommunications technology that is not utilized in a classroom convening on campus. Consequently, preparing to teach these courses has additional administrative and pedagogical considerations than its traditional on-campus equivalent. Administrative policies concerning intellectual property rights and course ownership are an integral component of teaching at a distance, especially when preparation is expected to include development of course content. Unlike a traditional course, teaching a distance education course will necessitate interaction with additional instructional technology support personnel who may work outside of the academic department.

Distance education technology can be either synchronous or asynchronous. Synchronous distance education technologies include Interactive Television (ITFS), Interactive video (ITV), or desktop videoconferencing. A synchronous course meets at a designated time in multiple locations that are closer to the student than commuting to the main campus. Face-to-face interaction between students and instructor remains an integral component of synchronous courses. When comparing distance education technologies, those taught using synchronous technologies are most similar to the traditional on-campus course. Although some existing instructional materials from the traditional course can be reused, preparation time needs to include strategies to maintain interaction and the attention of the students located at the remote sites.

Asynchronous distance education technologies (telecourse,

Internet, CD-ROM) which are characterized by anytime, any-place learning, provide flexibility and convenience for both students and instructors. With an asynchronous course, there is no designated class meeting time or classroom, but students can access instructional materials anytime and anyplace as long as a computer or television and videocassette recorder are available. Students and instructor interact primarily using computer-mediated technology, such as desktop videoconferencing, and text-based communication tools, such as e-mail and threaded discussions.

Institution will differ in their investment in distance education technologies, directly impacting opportunities for securing a distance education assignment. Inquire about the college and/or academic department's mission, vision, strategic plan or priorities, which address commitment to advancing distance education opportunities by targeting specific programs or degrees. Find out the technologies currently in use and future plans for expanding to other available technologies. Determine if there is a match between your personal interest and potential distance education assignment at the college.

Prior to accepting the assignment, thoroughly understand the institution's intellectual property and ownership policy for course development. Institutions vary on compensation for development of distance education courses and ownership rights. Some institutions rely on "work for hire" policies. This means that work done by a faculty member under contract belongs to the institution. Other institutions have policies that include joint ownership and revenue sharing, similar to patent agreements. At other times, the faculty can negotiate to retain all copyrights—even of instructional materials (Boettcher, 1999). Cash, release time, or hiring on-campus faculty on an overload basis are all possibilities for course development.

Identify the instructional technology resources and their respective services for each delivery medium available to the campus. Although there may be a departmental colleague teaching at a distance, get the campus-wide or academic unit's perspective on the course development process and design standards. The "Lone Ranger" approach occurs in many institutions as faculty, student webmasters and a few isolated departments or colleagues attempt to create on-line courses. Many can yield good results, but the institution's ability to scale efforts, maintain quality courses and programs, and provide benefits to many other units in the institution is impossible using this approach (Hartman, Truman, 1997). A new trend in distance education course design is to use a systematic approach to course development which includes participating on a team that includes other resources like experts in the areas of the design and development of instructional materials, technology support and collegial content experts.

Irrespective of the delivery method, teaching with distance education technology requires advanced planning and preparation. Depending on the delivery medium, it may also require additional training and development of course materials. As mentioned earlier, there are pedagogical issues to consider when designing new instructional materials for a distance education course. Distance learning requires three things not always found in traditional classroom teaching: a) learner-centered design, b) learner-centered delivery skills, and c) direct learner participation (Ostendorf, 1997). New instructional strategies will need to be integrated into the design of course materials which focus on student-centered learning.

Seek and take advantage of training opportunities, both in and outside of the educational institution, to learn more about distance education technologies. Training may include seminars and workshops focusing on a particular distance delivery medium or on strategies for course development. Learn about any software and hardware standards in place for course design and development. In addition to the technical skills required to operate the equipment or software specific to the medium, competencies for distance teaching include course planning and organization, verbal and nonverbal presentation skills, collaborative teamwork, questioning strategies, subject matter expertise, student involvement and coordination of their activities at field sites (Cyrs, 1997).

Develop course materials with interactivity in mind. Irrespective of the delivery medium, interaction is important. How this is accomplished directly depends on the delivery medium. Moore (1989) identifies three types of interactions:

- interactions that occur between the **learner and the instructor,**
- interactions that occur **among learners,** and
- interactions that take place **between learners and the content** they are trying to master.

Interactions enable active learner participation in the instructional/ training/performance improvement process. They allow learners to tailor learning experiences to meet their specific needs or abilities. Interactions enable clarification and transfer of new ideas to already held concept frameworks. Interactions promote intrinsic motivation on the part of a learner by highlighting the relevance that new information may have under these circumstances (Wagner, 1997). When designing instructional strategies for distant students, the following types of interactions should be considered, interactions:

- to increase **participation,**
- to develop **communication,**
- to receive **feedback,**
- to enhance **elaboration and retention,**
- to support learner **control/self-regulation,**
- to increase **motivation,**
- for **negotiation and clarification** of understanding,
- for **team building,** and
- for **discovery and exploration.**

Request information about course evaluation processes for the students, course and instructor. Gain an understanding of long standing policies concerning proctored examinations requirements or on-line testing procedures. For course evaluations, the academic department may use the same criteria and forms used in the traditional course, along with an addendum to accommodate the use of technology and delivery medium. Conversely, there may be a completely distinct evaluation process. Track ongoing, informal feedback from students for future or immediate revisions of course materials. The first time a course is delivered, there are bound to be some glitches. Be sure to test developed course materials from the student's perspective prior to allowing student access. Problems requiring few resources, which can be resolved quickly, should take priority. Proactively keep the students informed about any problems or changes to previously communicated syllabus and weekly schedule information.

The ever increasing availability of distance education programs and courses will simultaneously increase opportunities for teaching assignments. These assignments will may include a mixture of traditional and distance education courses. While there are some similarities between these delivery mediums, the primary difference is that distance education courses will require more advance preparation and up-front information gathering to gain an understanding of the institution's administrative policies governing their distance education courses. Although instruction using distance education technologies may initially require more time, ultimately the instructor will benefit as expectations and roles are clarified, resulting in an effective and efficient course design, development and delivery.

References

Boettcher, J. V. (1999). Copyright and intellectual property. *Syllabus,* 34-36.

Cyrs, T. E. (1997). Competence in teaching at a distance. *Teaching and learning at a distance: What it takes to effectively to design, deliver and evaluate programs.* San Francisco: Jossey-Bass.

Hartman, J. L. & Truman B. E. (1997). *Going virtual: Lessons learned.* Paper presented at the CAUSE '97 Conference, Orlando, FL.

Moore, M. G. (1989, April). *Three modes of interaction. A presentation of the NUCEA forum: Issues in instructional interactivity.* Paper presented at annual meeting of National University Continuing Education Association, Salt Lake City, UT .

Ostendorf, V. A. (1997). Teaching by television. *Teaching and learning at a distance: What it takes to effectively to design, deliver and evaluate programs.* San Francisco: Jossey-Bass.

Wagner, E. D. (1997). Interactivity: From agents to outcomes. *Teaching and learning at a distance: What it takes to effectively design, deliver and evaluate programs.* San Francisco: Jossey-Bass.

Tinnie A. Banks is Instructional Design Media Coordinator, Lorain County Community College, Elyria, OH.

TOPIC XVII:

Testing and Test Strategies

By M. B. McKinley

It is an academic truism that classroom tests may be considered further learning experiences, as well as a differential measure of "learning/knowledge." To enhance the "learning" features that can occur with multiple-choice tests, the following represent three testing/learning-enhanced strategies:

1. provide students with the opportunity to use a **personal dictionary** while taking the test;

2. allow **"crib notes"** be used during the test and/or

3. permit **textbook use** for "open book" tests.

First, encourage students to bring a personal dictionary to the test so that they may look up any words they do not fully comprehend. In surveying students who have used the dictionary during tests, it was found that the words most commonly looked up are those of a general vocabulary kind. In other words, while they may look up technical vocabulary pertinent to course content, most use the dictionary for everyday words, e.g. ambiguity, complimentary, virtually, condone, delete, etc.

The major thrust of the use of a dictionary is that it enhances test validity. It may be reasonably assumed that students come to the test with varying levels of vocabulary sophistication—the use of a dictionary tends to flatten out these differences. Students who miss a particular test item can then be assumed to have erred because of lack of content knowledge and not because of a less sophisticated general vocabulary. After all, test validity means assessing course-related material, not upbringing—learned or otherwise.

A second strategy that can supplement learning in a multiple-choice testing environment is the use of "crib notes"—self-written notes designed to aid the student in answering test questions. One method of doing crib notes is to offer the student the opportunity to write anything and everything they can on both sides of a 5" x 8" index card and bring that single card to the test. Students who have participated in this testing strategy have reported almost universal endorsement of the idea. The most commonly cited benefit of the crib notes was that preparing the notes by looking for critical concepts, ideas, terms, etc. forced the student to analyze and synthesize information to a far greater degree than "just memorizing the material."

A third assessment approach that can be considered a further learning aid in a testing environment is to give "open-book" tests. Open book tests more closely resemble the real world outside the hallowed halls of academia. Effective problem solving and associated learning in the working world requires that successful persons know where and how to use the resources available—the textbook is a perfect resource for test taking! Some clear advantages that accrue to open-book testing:

1. students **rely less on memorizing facts and rely more on learning**, understanding, retaining, and applying concepts and principles;

2. students with abilities other than rote learning will have **a more equalized opportunity to succeed**; and

3. test questions can more **readily measure syntheses, analyses,** and allow for judgments.
    Note: Some faculty will protest that with an open book test students will not come to class. Not true, a student simply does not have the time to look up "everything" during the test and the instructor can include in lectures and discussions material that will be on the test as well.

An instructor may use all three of the testing strategies noted above or any combination thereof. For example, an instructor may have students use the "crib notes" along with a personal dictionary, thereby "doubling" the advantages over just one technique. Regardless of which ideas are used there are some general issues involving these testing strategies.

Student anxiety is a well-documented inhibitor of optimum test performance. Students have forever complained about the frustration and lack of control they feel in testing situations. If students feel such lack of control and the optimum test performance is inhibited, then the validity of the test is called into question. Students with an increased sense of well-being (less anxiety/frustration) as provided by the three assessment strategies, will in all likelihood do better on the tests, and more importantly, learn during the test. However and relatedly, faculty will be required to construct or select from test banks a better grade of questions to realize the maximum benefits of these alternative testing formats.

There is one great unanswered question remaining and that is:

> **Is the opportunity for student dishonesty during the test (cheating) more likely with any or all of these testing strategies?**

It has been the author's experience in having used all three testing formats that there is no known increased likelihood of academic dishonesty. After all, the dictionary, crib-notes and/or open books legitimately provide the resources that students might otherwise be tempted to use dishonestly. Indeed, a strong case can be made that the use of such techniques have, in actuality, reduced the motivation to "cheat" as the student thinks the testing strategy is more compassionate, just and fair.

A final note on multiple-choice tests themselves. Whether an instructor creates his or her own test questions from "scratch" or selects questions from a test bank, there are a number of points to keep in mind so that the resultant test works in achieving its intended purpose(s) regardless of the testing strategy employed. Here is a short list of some of those points:

1. Do **questions relate to a learning outcome(s)?**

2. **Are the questions written in "correct" English,** e.g. a/an before a vowel?

3. **Have the foils (answers) been arranged in a systematic fashion,** such as alphabetically or length of answer?

4. **Are correct answers roughly balanced** as to the number of A's, B's, C's and D's?

5. **Have negative questions been avoided?** Or, if used (sparingly!), has the negative been underlined or bolded?

6. Does the **test start with a couple of confidence-building questions?**

7. **Are there some "humorous" items scattered throughout the test** as anxiety reducers?

8. **Are some items personalized,** e.g. identifies the instructor with the material, class?

9. Have **so-called "tricky" items been avoided?**

Ideally, multiple-choice questions should be geared to take about 45 seconds per question and the questions themselves should not be comprised of more than four foils each—a fifth foil detracts from test validity!

All in all, the author has been using a combination of the above noted testing strategies over many years and while no single one of the techniques works best in all situations, each has proved its worth in some circumstances. From most quarters then, such strategies may work for some testing environs. Come to think of it, there is little or no reason the three strategies can not be used in an essay test mode, is there?

Dr. M. B. McKinley is Professor of Psychology, Lorain County Community College, Elyria, OH.

TOPIC XVIII:

Testing and Grading

By Donald Grieve

One of the most important aspects of a student's education is the testing and grading practices of the instructor. Too often students taking their courses are conditioned to the sole purpose of trying to determine the responses wanted on the instructor's tests. In addition to student evaluation, the testing process should also be an evaluation of instruction and improvement in the teaching/learning situation. It is important that the testing process incorporate a strategy of reinforcing student successes and positive experiences as well as identifying weaknesses. Unfortunately, in the past, testing was used for a variety of purposes that often raised the anxieties of the students. This included the elimination of students from more difficult and demanding programs, disciplines, and courses as well as to rank students for class standing and scholarship qualifications. These and other factors have a direct effect upon student behaviors, including anxiety, during the testing process.

It is important that you as the instructor make every effort to prepare students at the beginning of the course for your testing plan. This starts by informing students on the first day of the class of the testing procedure that you will use, the times that tests will be given, and the content (determined by class objectives) upon which the students will be tested. This avoids the age-old complaint of students that "he or she didn't test over what they talked about in class".

In summary, the ideal reasons that tests are given should be:

1. to reveal to students their areas of strengths and success,

---

2. to indicate to the instructor the students' progress,

3. to provide motivation for students,

4. to help instructors evaluate their teaching,

5. to provide a basis upon which grades are determined, and

6. to evaluate students in terms of their professional and career goals.

Too often students and faculty consider testing as a process to determine grades alone when in fact there are more lasting reasons for testing.

As a teacher you are experienced and familiar with the major types of tests. You have both participated in these tests as a student and have administered them as an instructor. The most commonly used tests in the past were essay and recall tests. However, with the advent of computerized scoring and the gathering of statistical data, the multiple-choice test has become increasingly popular. At the college level these has been little attention given to performance tests, oral tests, written tests, or short answer tests. For that reason the major emphasis in this section will be descriptions of the tests that are used most extensively.

Achievement Tests

Nearly all of the tests that you will administer while teaching your course can be classified as achievement tests. Although some instructors use ungraded or even oral quizzes to add to the learning situation, they are usually given to provide learning experiences rather than evaluation. Occasionally, you may be called upon to administer a standardized achievement test which has been developed by a commercial agency, the department or discipline, or other entities. However, this discussion is dedicated primarily to the instructor's construction of classroom tests.

It is difficult to develop a good testing instrument that measures more than rote knowledge or regurgitation of notes the student has taken. Ideally, a properly constructed classroom test would determine the student growth in the cognitive, psychomotor, and affective domains. Achievement tests are developed in many formats. The most basic achievement test, of course, is the written response. The most common tests known to faculty—multiple-choice, essay, and true/false—are all achievement tests. This section will address primarily these test types. Before continuing with the discussion of tests, however, it is important that we first discuss two important characteristics of good tests, *validity* and *comprehensiveness.*

Test Validity

The validity of a test is determined by answering the very simple question, "Am I testing what I should be testing?" Probably in many of the classes that you attended as an undergraduate, the validity of the tests were in question. Too often course preparations were not structured in a way that testing was consistent with the discussions that took place in the class or in the course objectives. This very often happens in classes where instructors use tests over and over. In modern class planning, which requires that each course has objectives, validity becomes less of a problem. To maintain validity in a testing situation, you must be certain that your evaluation instrument and questions on it are based upon the objectives written for the course.

Test Comprehensiveness

Obviously, the comprehensiveness of a test is important in evaluating students. A test that is not comprehensive will be neither valid nor objective. To test students on a small sample of what has been taught during the course is unfair to students who may not completely grasp that segment of the course, but have mastery over the class in general. *Again, comprehensiveness is not a problem if objectives are written to cover a broad spectrum of the major purposes of the course and the test is developed from those objectives.* You must be careful to make certain that the test adequately samples all the content which has been taught. The development of a broad body of questions, covering the entire course and then selecting from those questions at evaluation time, can assure comprehensiveness without repetition of questions.

Essay Tests

Essay tests are still one of the most popular colleges tests. They are effective at any level of the learning hierarchy. That is, analysis and synthesis are usually incorporated into the essay questions. Although essay tests require considerable time for students to respond, they do give an in-depth perspective of overall student ability. In keeping with the andragogical model discussed earlier in this publication, the essay test is an excellent opportunity for you to interact directly and personally with students. Essay tests can be returned with comments and suggestions and can incorporate creativity, problem solving, and critical thinking skills. Essay tests give significant insight into what the students are learning and what they are hearing in the classroom.

There are several factors to remember when writing test questions that require essay answers. First and foremost is that essay questions should be related to the written course objectives. They should, if possible, be related to the objectives at the analysis or synthesis level. Secondly, essay questions should incorporate a significant amount of content. Realizing that the students will take a long time to respond, questions should be worded so that excessive time is not spent on trivial matters. Finally, you must be certain that in terms of vocabulary, content, and subject covered, the student has sufficient background to respond adequately to the question being asked and that the question is not ambiguous or deceptive.

Essay questions, if constructed and graded properly, are the most accurate of the possible testing techniques. In recent years, despite most teachers resorting to some type of objective grading system, the essay question still leaves considerable latitude for students of ability to express themselves beyond the minimum required competencies. Although this also runs the risk of allowing professional jargon, it usually allows some degree of objectiveness and can be used in a positive manner if controlled by the objectives of the course. Individuals who develop a high degree of skill in writing essay questions find that they can allow for a degree of flexibility.

Grading essay questions presents the greatest problem. You must keep in mind that essay questions are asking students to be objective, yet to generalize. The appropriate way to judge an essay response is to write the response from a faculty viewpoint, listing important comments in priority. Assigning points to the prioritized criteria will then lead to a degree of grading objectivity. You must be cautious, however, that essay questions do not ask for student opinions. Theoretically, if one is merely asking for an opinion, every student should get a perfect score.

Advantages of Essay Questions

There are numerous advantages as well as disadvantages in testing using essay questions. The most obvious advantages are:

1. They **provide in-depth coverage of material or content** presented in the class.

2. They **allow students maximum utilization of their capabilities** in responding to an issue.

3. They **are quick and simple to prepare**.

4. They **can be changed from class to class** without greatly affecting the purpose of the question.

Disadvantages of Essay Questions

The disadvantages of testing using essay questions are:

1. They **restrict measurable subject matter.**
2. They **are time consuming for students.**
3. They **have a tendency to weigh too heavily a specific part of the course** at the expense of other parts.
4. They **present the burden of handwriting, spelling, vocabulary, and grammar** upon the student.
5. They **have a tendency toward subjectivity** in evaluation.
6. They **are difficult to grade.**

Multiple-choice Tests

With the advent of computerized scoring and large classes, multiple-choice tests probably are the most predominately used tests in college classrooms today. Not only has the influx of large class instruction and differing class sizes nearly mandated the use of a quickly graded objective system, the capability of providing statistical analysis concerning individual questions is easily obtained from a computerized multiple-choice test. In fact, computer programs exist which allow the instructor to change multiple-choice tests for different classes of the same course. This is accomplished by developing a large database of questions and randomly selecting from the database.

Multiple-choice tests are valuable in that they can measure discrimination abilities between answers as well as simple knowledge. Students with poor handwriting or verbal abilities are not burdened by these unrelated factors which might alter their grades otherwise.

The development of multiple-choice questions is not a simple matter. First, the multiple-choice question should deal with a significant aspect of the course and not be general in nature. You must be careful not to include what may be interpreted as "trick" or misleading questions. It is also important that words not be used in the question that are not understood by all students in the course. Also, present the multiple-choice question in a positive rather than a negative manner.

The actual construction of the multiple-choice tests has several general guidelines. They include:

- do not include answers that are obviously correct or incorrect,

- be sure the correct answers are scattered throughout the response mechanism,

- have no more than four alternative answers with the possibility being right,

- do not use "all of the above" or "none of the above", and

- do not use the terms never, always, likely, or similar adjectives that may divert the meaning for the student.

Advantages of Multiple-choice Tests

In deciding the type of question to use for your evaluation tests, you must consider the advantages and disadvantages. The advantages of multiple-choice questions are:

1. They **can cover a broad scope of work** in a short time.

2. They measure the **abilities of students to recognize appropriate responses** rather than recall facts. (This is a significant benefit to older students who sometimes may have difficulty recalling things that they have learned).

3. They are **more valid than some other kinds of tests** and can be easily statistically checked for validity.

4. Students can be **tested at the analysis and synthesis level**.

5. They are **easy to grade**.

6. They **are easily made comprehensive** in nature.

Disadvantages of Multiple-choice Tests
The disadvantages of multiple-choice questions are:

1. There is a **tendency to construct most responses** toward the learned knowledge.

2. The **questions are time consuming and difficult to develop** if validity is maintained.

3. They **provide for guessing and elimination of responses**.

4. They **rely primarily upon recall and memory** and not problem solving and critical thinking.

Short Answer and Recall Tests

The compromise between the multiple-choice test and the essay test is the short answer or the recall test. Short-answer questions can provide students with the opportunity to show their knowledge of a presentation, simulation, or analogy. They can be written to a specific item or point and thus do not require the time and effort involved in essay questions. They allow the student to use creativity and analysis that is not permissible with the multiple-choice test. The short answer and recall tests provide the instructor with the opportunity to pose simple questions or even completion questions. They provide the opportunity for expansion of creative ideas and expression of philosophies and opinions. They also provide the student with the opportunity to discuss unassigned material or materials they may have used on a research project or paper associated with the course. Short answer questions or recall questions may provide the student the opportunity to present the solution to problems or to develop hypothesis. Such questions may allow students to compare the differences between two statements, items, or activities which is not possible in the use of many other tests.

The Advantages of Recall Tests

The advantages of recall tests are:

1. They are **relatively simply to grade and construct.**

2. Recall questions **can address numerous areas and a broad field of content.**

3. They **require a specific recall** rather than a guess such as may occur in a true/false or multiple-choice.

Disadvantages of Recall Tests

The disadvantages of recall tests include:

1. They may be **time consuming for the student** in terms of thinking and trying to recall something for which they have a mental block.

2. **Subjectivity may be introduced** due to similar responses.

3. It is **nearly impossible to measure analysis or synthesis** with these tests.

True/False Tests

True/false questions are not commonly used at the college level any longer. Although they may have their place in a sampling of student responses or learning activity, they generally are not acceptable as being objective or valid. In the event there is opportunity for their use, the advantages, disadvantages, and some suggestions are listed below.

Advantages of True/False Questions

1. **A large number of diverse questions may be asked on a specific topic.**

2. They are good **to stimulate students and give lower ability students** a chance for success.

3. They are **simple and time saving to develop**.
4. They are **valid as only two possible answers** exist.
5. They are **non-threatening and familiar** to students.
6. They are **easily scored**.

Disadvantages of True/False Questions
1. Even with the allowance for correction factors, true/false questions **encourage guessing**.
2. It is **difficult to construct brief, complete true/false statements** where the answer is not obvious.
3. **Grading weight is equal for minor as well as significant items**.
4. They are **not appropriate for elaboration or discussion**.
5. They **tend to test the lower level of knowledge** with no consideration for analysis and synthesis.
6. They are **typically low in validity and reliability** due to the guess factor.

Constructing True/False Test Items
If you have elected to utilize true/false questions as part of your evaluation system, there are several factors to consider in the development of these questions. They are:

1. **Avoid unclear statements** with ambiguous words or "trick" questions.
2. **Develop questions that require responses beyond** the knowledge or rote memorization level.
3. **Avoid patterning answers** with a long string of trues or false or direct alteration.
4. **Avoid direct quotes** as they will tip off responses.
5. **Avoid specific descriptors or adjectives** that tip off responses.

Grading

Assignment of grades is probably the most difficult task of teaching. All of the elements of teaching (preparation, presentation, and student activity) are reflected in the grading process. In addition, in an era of accountability, teachers are sometimes called upon to justify grades with documentation. Thus the establishment of firm criteria for grading is necessary. There are some general rules that are helpful in establishing the grading process. They are as follows:

1. **Communicate criteria.** Faculty should communicate the grading criteria to be used the first or second session of class. A suggested chart for this activity is shown in figure 1. Every effort should be made to allow students to respond to the grading format in the process, before the first evaluation is given.

2. **Include criteria other than test scores.** Factors other than test scores should be included in the students' grades. This is especially true of social sciences courses where content criteria and problem solving is not easy to assess. For example, if it is important for students to communicate or express ideas, then class participation *should* be a part of the grading criteria. If a paper or a project is part of the grade, students should be advised of the weight of the project applied to the grade. If laboratory demonstration is part of the course, the grade value should be made known.

3. **Avoid irrelevant factors.** Avoid introducing irrelevant factors to the grading process. Including attendance and tardiness in the grading criteria is unwise. Many experienced teachers feel that if students possess knowledge and show that they have reached the objectives of the course, they should be evaluated on that criteria only. The insistence that students should sit in the room for a certain number of minutes to hear things they already know may be unrealistic. This is especially true when

teaching adults who may have significant career and business experience but have not received the official credit or coursework. Introducing attendance in class as part of the grading criteria simply breeds animosity with students and is very difficult for the instructor to justify.

4. **Weigh grading criteria carefully.** Be careful not to weight certain segments of the grading criteria inappropriately. For example, if you are to develop a grading plan such as shown in the diagram in figure 1, and then allow 90% of the grade to count as the final examination, you have probably defeated the purpose of comprehensive grading. Equally important is the weighing of extra credit for extra work. If such a technique is used it should not penalize students who do not feel it necessary to do extra work.

5. **Grade students on their achievement, not on other students.** Grading should be based upon the criteria of the course objectives and not upon other students' scores. Many years ago, teachers used the technique of "grading on the curve." This technique essentially distributed all students and all classes on a normal bell curve and determined the percentage of A's, B's, C's, and D's. This placed students in competition with each other rather than cooperating in the learning experience. The practice has been abandoned in the modern classroom. In recent years, criterion-based grading has found favor. Criterion-based grading evaluates students independent of other students based upon the criteria of the course. The criteria of the course are the objectives written for the course. Thus, quite simply the student should be graded upon the degree upon which they have completed the objectives of the course and not how other students achieve. Thus, if all students reach all objectives they all should receive passing grades.

Evaluation Plan

In order to clearly delineate criteria for assignment of grades, it is helpful if you first develop an evaluation plan. An evaluation plan is a very simple device used to develop a short worksheet form. The plan contains all of the factors that apply to the evaluation of the students. Across from these factors is listed a percentage of weight that will be assigned to various factors. A third column indicates the points received for each factor. A sample plan is shown in figure 1.

Evaluation Chart

Grade Factors	Percentage of Final Grade	Possible Points	Points Received
Tests	60	90	————
Paper	20	30	————
Project	10	10	————
Class Participation	10	15	————
TOTALS	100	150	————

Figure 1—Evaluation Chart Sample

Please note that any number of factors can be included in the first column. For example, a technical course might include laboratory work, laboratory demonstrations, or completion of projects. An evaluation worksheet allows you to weight factors that apply to a specific class with the flexibility of changing them when necessary. Obviously when developing the chart, it is necessary that the weight total 100% for the course. In order to complete the evaluation worksheet, you must simply assign the number of points possible to each of the categories. Keep in mind that the total number of points may not equal 100, depending upon the application involved. (Example shows 150.) It remains then to simply add a fourth column titled "points received". Points received, obviously, are the number of points earned by the student in each category.

This system allows you the flexibility of established documented criteria for the assignment of grades. You may, for example, arbitrarily put the total number of points desired to equal 100%. This then can be converted to the number of points necessary to be earned through each of the factors by multiplying by the percentage. An additional step is to simply take that number of points divided by the number of activities in each of the factors to determine the value for each activity, even to the level of determining the value of each test question. This documentation clearly indicates to the students the process by which evaluation is conducted in a businesslike and professional manner.

Item Analysis

A quick and relatively scientific method of checking the validity of exam questions is to utilize the technique of item analysis. Although appearing cumbersome and labor intensive at an initial glance, item analysis is not a complex activity. Keep in mind that item analysis will be applied to only those questions that need analysis or checks on their validity. Therefore, in most testing situations the process will be applied to approximately five to ten percent of the questions. Item analysis allows you to check, on the basis of performance, the validity of questions by determining if students who received highest scores on the total test were successful in obtaining the correct answer on the questions being analyzed. Figure 2 shows a chart indicating how item analysis is performed.

Item Analysis Chart

Question No. _____

Response	A	B	C	D	F
Correct					
Incorrect					

Figure 2—Item Analysis Chart Sample

This chart shows the responses of students who received A's, B's, C's or D's across the top of the chart. The left hand column shows which of the students achieved the correct answer to the question and which ones responded with the incorrect answer. In order to perform item analysis, you must record in the appropriate space the information for which the chart asks. That is, how many A students responded with the correct answer and how many responded incorrectly. This process is continued until all possible combinations are exhausted. Obviously, from this point on, you can become as statistically sophisticated as you wish. Correlations, percentages, etc. can be determined. The bottom line, however, is simply to answer this question: Did students who received high percentage scores on the total test also respond in a similar percentage of correct answers on the questions analyzed. Obviously, if the A students received 90% correct answers and above and only 50% correct responses on the questions being analyzed it could be assumed it probably is not a valid question.

Item analysis is a simple technique quickly conducted and probably underutilized. It is a very simple process to determine the validity of questionable test items and provides you the opportunity to reword or rephrase the question so that it more accurately reflects the intent. As was indicated earlier, the simple process described here is not intended to be statistically foolproof, however, it is certainly an improvement over the possibility of guessing when considering such validity, or worse, the possibility of leaving an invalid question or series of questions in an otherwise effective instrument.

Dr. Don Greive is author/editor and consultant for adjunct faculty programs.

TOPIC XIX:

Classroom Applications: Miscellaneous Topics

The following articles are discipline specific and written by practicing adjunct faculty members and some of those who work with them at a variety of colleges and universities. Many of the items have previously appeared in *Adjunct Info-A Journal for Managers of Adjunct and Part-time Faculty*. I am grateful to the authors for their permission to reprint the articles in this publication.

Donald Greive, Editor
Info-Tec
Elyria, Ohio

• •

This Class Scares Me!

"I put this class off 'til the last semester!" "I am a pretty good writer, I just don't want to get up in front of folks to deliver what I wrote!" "I really dread this class!"

These are comments I hear at the beginning of every class, every term. These comments are made by students aged 18 to 45, first-time college students, and veteran college students. Our textbook says that fear of public speaking is the second ranking anxiety producer to "a party of strangers." To help demystify this common baggage, I start the first night of Public Speaking 2600 with an approach the gives the students some safety and some connections to their own lives.

The Galef Institute, headquartered in Los Angeles, advocates that:

    ❧ **Students learn what matters to them,**
The most significant learning arises from that which
arouses the interest and meets the needs of the learner.

    ❧ **Students construct meaning for themselves,** and
The most significant and enduring learning is constructed
by the learner, not imposed from without. Students learn
best when they are engaged in controlling their own
learning.

    ❧ **Students thrive in a safe, supportive environment.**
Begin with students' strengths, celebrate all they can do,
and encourage them to build from there.

Those theories form the underpinnings for curriculum content
and an approach to teaching that Galef calls "Different Ways of
Knowing". I find these theories to be truths for all learners at all
ages. I try to be mindful of these theories as I teach on the college
level.

I have found a strategy that is helpful for introducing the whole
"package" of public speaking. To provide a safe environment for
learners to construct their own meaning and to provide a window
for learners to see how the subject matters to them, I start with
what they know.

After general first night housekeeping chores, I divide the
class into six groups. Each group is given a page with one question on it. They are to discuss, argue, and brainstorm answers
then have a reporter share their ideas with the whole class. The
questions are:

1. Why are most people afraid of public speaking?

2. What elements are similar in conversation and public
speaking?

3. What is the difference between conversation and public
speaking?

4. What makes it hard for you to listen to a speaker?

5. What kind of speaker holds your interest?

6. What causes you to be persuaded—to buy something,

to try something, to change your mind?

When these groups share their thoughts and we chart them for all to see—I am honestly able to say to them, "You have identified all the topics we will deal with in this class. You already know a great deal about what comprises an effective and non-effective speech." The students have had an opportunity to be successful on their first night of class, some community and safety has been established, and they are thinking how public speaking is already a part of their lives.

I am sure this tool could be used for any subject. It is an effective way to get instant feedback on how knowledgeable students are. I also think it is more effective to have students focus on specific questions than to just use the K/W/L chart. (Ask students to list "What do you *Know*?" "What do you *Want* to know?", and at the end of the term, "What did you *Learn*?")

Perhaps if the "dreaded last semester class" can begin with a supportive environment, it can ease students into expressing information, opinions, and ideas from other areas of their lives.

Contributed by: Harolyn Sharpe of Florida Community College, Jacksonville, FL.

● ●

Named After a Saint:

Free Writing in the College Classroom

It took me a long time to ask my father one simple question: Would he be hurt if I legally changed my middle name when I turned eighteen? He was quiet for several minutes, time I spent worrying, Did I totally offend him? Then finally, he asked, "Exactly what is your middle name?"

My sister and I have told this story many times since then, but every time I tell it I am reminded of how important our names are. As an adjunct professor at five colleges in the Seacoast region of New Hampshire and southern Maine, I teach approximately two classes every eight weeks. Most classes are about 20 students, and it is next to impossible for me to remember students' names, especially unusual names or names I find hard to pronounce. Because I try to learn names by week two, I have to employ a variety of techniques to be successful.

My most successful name activity came from my colleague Jennifer Miller who, near the start of each semester, asks students to free write about their names: what it means, how they feel about it, and how they got it. After the free writing time is up, Jennifer asks her students to read their free writing out loud.

When this fairly painless activity is over, I've accomplished several things. First of all, most students will read this free write out loud; it's a safe topic about which they are an expert. So, right from the first week of classes, they have participated. And what's more—this activity can be easily reworked, depending on the class. In my business communications classes, instead of a free writing activity, I ask students to write me a properly formatted memo about their names. In my composition classes, stories from this activity often turn into personal narratives.

This activity also gives me an opportunity to connect with students over a non-graded piece of writing. At the end of the class, I collect these free writes, and write lots of encouraging comments on them. (Since they are free writes, I don't check for spelling, grammar, structure—all that stuff). My goal is to set a tone for the semester, especially in my larger classes where I may not get to talk one-on-one with my students frequently.

And the bottom line is that I learn something about my students, something I can use to remember names. One student wrote, "It's fair to say I don't just dislike my full given name, I cringe at it." Another hates her name because when it's said fast with a New England accent it sounds like "calamari." Another student was supposed to be a boy—disappointed she wasn't, her parents simply added an "a" to the first and middle names they had picked for their "son." Yet another student, last in a long line of kids, was named after a character in a movie. "There are seven children, so I would assume it was tougher after the first few," my student wrote, "my middle name, Joseph, was given for religious reasons. Each of my siblings also have (sic) middle names that are names of saints in the Catholic church."

Catholic saint-inspired or not, my students' names stick with me as the short semester swirls by, thanks to their free writes. Indeed, maybe I should suggest this activity to my father ... but then again, I think I've tortured him enough.

Contributed by: **Darcy Wakefield** *of Southern Maine Technical College, Portland, ME.*

●●●●●●●●●●●●●●●●●●●●●●●●●●●●●●●●●●●●●●●

The First Class: What to do after the Introductions

After all the preparation and trepidation, the "big moment" arrives—the first class. Beyond knowledge of the content and of teaching strategies, here are some general recommendations to apply to that first class. Most of the recommendations focus upon classroom management strategies that can apply to any level of instruction.

To be successful on the first day, **BE ORGANIZED.**

1. **Organize your presentation.** Prepare a step-by-step outline to prompt you. Use media support, such as a PowerPoint™ presentation to keep yourself on track.

2. **Organize your materials.** Prepare your handout materials, such as your syllabus, prior to the first class. Ensure that they are copied in time and ready to distribute during the first class. Distribute the materials in a planned and deliberate fashion, not as an afterthought.

3. **Organize your environment.** If you require audiovisual/multimedia equipment, make certain that it is

scheduled and available. If you want to rearrange the classroom, do so prior to the class (if the room is not in use) or at the beginning of the class as students arrive.

4. **Organize your "Class Procedures."** If assigned seating is important to you, start the procedure during the first class. If homework assignments should be submitted at the beginning (or end) of the class into a "Homework Folder," inform the students.

And don't forget to **BE OPTIMISTIC**.

1. **Maintain optimism and a good attitude** toward your teaching and your students.

2. **Learn something about the students.** Have the students complete a form, sharing information (such as their major, favorite book, goals for enrolling in the class.) The activity can lessen their apprehension, as well as assist you in learning their names. It may also aid you in identifying student goals or needs.

You must have everything ready to go when class begins. Your success during the school year will be determined by what you do during the first class after the introductions.

Contributed by: **Swen H. DiGranes** *of Northeastern State University, Tahlequah, OK and* **Jo Lynn Autry DiGranes** *of Connors State College, Warner and Muskogee, OK.*

• •

Critical Writing Tips

I use the following guidelines in all my courses and attach then to each of my syllabi:

Critical writing is a form of critical thinking. If you are clear about your ideas, you should be able to write them clearly and coherently. If your ideas are vague or confused, your writing will not magically clarify them. Do not assume that the reader will know what you meant to say. If your writing is poor then your ideas will be poorly expressed and poorly understood. Do not assume that substantive ideas and strong content can overcome poor expression and weak writing.

- ❧ **Identify topic, purpose, and conclusion clearly**— write a statement for each prior to writing your paper, essay, etc.

- ❧ **Outline** (use style of your choosing): **Include introduction** (purpose and what will be done), **body and conclusion** (either a summary or the conclusion of the argument, depending on the approach you use.)

- ❧ **Free write or brainstorm for ideas BUT do not submit this material.** Use only as a source of ideas and issues.

- ❧ **Identify key concepts and ideas.** Make sure they are clearly stated and provide clear relationships between and among them.

- ❧ **Check for unwarranted assumptions** (e.g. "All laws are morally good"), **faulty facts** (e.g. "Being old means a person loses interest in sexual activity"), **or poor inferences** (e.g. "Two men holding hands means they are gay").

- ❧ **Critically read your material looking for unanswered questions, views or positions** that can be challenged. Think about alternative positions to the ones you've stated and address the challenges to your ideas.

- ❧ **Provide some style in writing,** (e.g. varying sentence and paragraph length; using rich words and avoiding cliches; keeping language concrete and direct; avoiding trying to be overly impressive; avoiding repetition and expanding text with irrelevant or trivial material to meet a page requirement and avoiding passive voice—it usually leads to ambiguity).

- ❧ **Develop your ideas where necessary,** make sure ideas are explained fully, define all concepts, use illustrations or examples often, include detailed descriptions of primary points.

- ❧ **Formal writing is not equivalent to colloquial speaking.** Avoid:
  a. using less instead of fewer,
  b. the word "this" as a noun referring to some vague antecedent,
  c. incorrectly using such statements as "a person (which is singular) did their (which is plural) best..."
  d. using slang or contractions, unless for special effect.

- ❧ **Check grammar and spelling,** always have a dictionary or use "spell check" and keep a thesaurus available.

*Contributed by **Charles R. Schmidtke** of Canisus College, Buffalo, NY.*

• •

Speech Logs with a Twist

Goal: To foster critical thinking by defining, comprehending, applying and analyzing the concepts presented in a text.

As I was developing critical thinking ideas for my class, I came across the idea of the speech log. This idea intrigued me as I'd been looking for ways to incorporate writing into my class. To use this format, the instructor must review each chapter in the textbook to identify the concepts to be covered and make a guide listing the concepts by chapter. The students are asked to purchase a three-ring binder. Student divide a sheet of 8.5x11" paper down the center with a line. On the left side of the paper, the identified items and concepts are defined. Students number the concepts, writing or paraphrasing the definition from the book.

Once students have identified the concepts, the critical thinking begins! The first activity is the comprehension, application, and analysis of the information just defined. The students are provided with a list of sentence starters which help them comprehend, apply, and analyze the concepts, some examples are: "This concept will help my speeches by _____; I learned that _____; I like what I said about _____; I don't like what was said about _____." These starter sentences help guide and direct the students.

When students critique the concepts, it is important to stress that there is no right or wrong answer. They are to analyze and apply their material based on their experiences with other classes, their jobs, hobbies, and families. These critical thinking comments are written on the right side of their logs beside each item or concept previously defined. As a direct result of this assignment, another objective emerges for generating questions. As a part of the sentence starters, I've included question starters. Some examples are: "Why must we_____? What is so important about _____? How can we use _____ in our speeches?" And "How does _____ compare to _____?" To answer the questions and save myself hours of reading and writing, the students are assigned to groups in the class. They are asked to discuss their questions and generate answers. Questions the group cannot answer satisfactorily are collected and I use this to guide my discussion of the chapter that day. This method helps ensure the relevance of the information I present to students. This assignment has added a new dimension to my class. I highly recommend adding this to your course and predict you'll be intrigued by the students' responses.

*Contributed by: **John Stoebig** of College of the Sequoias, Visalia, CA.*

• •

Relevancy of Teaching Sociology

I teach sociology at Johnson and Wales University in Charleston, SC. Johnson and Wales is world renowned for its culinary school, for its excellent hotel and hospitality graduates. Ah-ha, so how do you teach students sociology, students interested in the hospitality business? They don't care that Auguste Comte was the father of sociology or the founder of positivism. How about the three major theories of sociology? Are they ever going to use that as a banquet manager?

No, no, no, but they need to learn it and learn it they will and most will leave loving the class for all it was. Some may remember Auguste Comte and some may not but they will have all have benefited from the boring drudgery of learning it. You see when it is boring factual material I spend a minimal amount of time lecturing about it, and I look for the relevancy of it and tell them to remember it as if they were going to be a contestant on *Jeopardy* or *Who Wants to Be a Millionaire*. These things become trivia questions in life. You will remember some of this and become the star of every cocktail party. You might even be the lifeline for the millionaire contest. Think of how proud everyone in your family will be when you are called and know the answer, especially if you're the G.M. of a Hyatt Regency. Wow.

So what DO I do? I explain first and foremost how sociology is the study of human behavior, and if human behavior doesn't interest you then you should not be in the hotel/hospitality industry. An industry that in itself is comprised of "thank you's" and "I'm sorry's", and if you say "I'm sorry" and "thank you" you must be saying it to someone, i.e. a human. This brings me to my point on relevancy. Things must be relevant or students are not interested. Even in the best of schools, students are looking for the relevancy in all subject matter. Am I ever going to use this? Do I need this? Do I even care about this?

There is a project in my class that counts for 20% of the grade, outside of tests. Students are asked to find an article each week for five weeks on the five topics I have selected and do a one-page article review on each. Aside from bring related to the chapter, it must be related to the hospitality, hotel, and travel/tourism business. Example: Chapter 10 is on social class, Weber, and the sociological twist on the importance of social classes, so students must find an article that discusses social class in the industry (i.e. hotels that are adding extra amenities to accommodate people who have more money, or hotels that are donating food to an organization to feed the homeless.)

Yes, they must learn the theories of sociology, and yes, they must know the names of the sociologists that proposed the theories, but they should also learn to love some aspect of sociology and see the relevancy. Because yes, you will use this in the future, and yes, you need this, and yes, you should care about this—and years from now when you're on a game show and someone asks you who the father of sociology was, you might say, "Hey, wait a minute, I do remember that. It was in this crazy class where the professor tried to show us the relevancy of all education in life." You think, you hesitate, you remember there's so much, but you take a breath and say, "Auguste Comte," and you're right. You win a million dollars, but you win more than that, you have won the ability to recall what you've learned because life is a series of game shows and one never knows when one needs to be prepared with the correct answer. So I think I'll donate that million to that crazy sociology professor that helped me remember the importance of all this.

*Contributed by: **Lisa Lend Cohen** of Johnson & Wales University, Charleston, SC.*

• •

Using Short Literature to Facilitate Learning

I teach Composition One as an adjunct for Florida Community College in Jacksonville, FL. The course includes learning different rhetorical modes such as narration and description. To augment my lectures, I give my classes hand-outs of short pieces published by famous authors to demonstrate the particular method of writing the class is examining. For instance, with discussion of narration, I might use a work from Maya Angelou's "Champion of the World", which tells of her childhood and growing up in the Pre-Civil Rights South. The point here is to get my students acquainted with an active telling of a tale which is central to all good narration.

After the students have read the short work in class, they break up into small groups of four or five and explore the piece through questions I provide. The discussion questions focus on the writing method we are discussing. Reading the story in class has several important advantages. In my experience, I have found that generally even well-prepared students are not always ready for class every day. Everyone has equal opportunity to read the story, so discussions are fresh and insightful. It does take some time away from lecture, but I think my students enjoy this process and learn more. I believe that students learn more from their peers, than they do from some "talking head" in front of a podium.

There is another advantage to this process. For many students this is their introduction to literature. By carefully selecting the pieces, I can broaden my students' familiarity with literature. Sometimes my students will then delve more deeply into the works of an author or two we have examined in class. In fact, frequently my students will ask me what other works a particular author has written. This activity is also in keeping with my department's directives to establish a broader base for reading activities in the classroom. This fits very neatly into a composition curriculum because no one can write well if he does not read well and often.

As a result of this activity, my students get a feel for each other and each other's ideas. My students enjoy a strong sense of bonding which makes the classroom environment all the more fun.

*Contributed by: **Cameron Chambers** of Florida Community College, Jacksonville, FL.*

"Dou wanna know how to talk?"

We Americans are very sloppy in our speech. We leave out letters and syllables, run words together, and mumble pronunciations. I imagine the first "street indoctrination" is very alarming for a person from another country learning our language. I can picture him or her running to the dictionary to look up "jeet" after hearing one American ask another, "Jeet yet?" Much of this sloppiness is bad habit, stemming from what we hear around us constantly. Think how consistently we all use "gonna."

In my Public Speaking class, I use two activities to sharpen students' enunciation and pronunciation. The first is an enunciation activity that actually grew out of work with elementary school students. Adults and children learn and giggle with this. I use a "call and response" exercise with a poem, where I say each line and the class repeats it. I speak in a rhythm and sometimes we snap our fingers! I ask them to exaggerate the consonant sounds and to speak with their mouths open.

> What did you put in your pocket?
> Your pickety pockety pocket?
> Early Monday morning?
>
> I put in chocolate ice cream
> Slurpy, glurpy ice cream
> Early Monday morning.
>
> What did you put in your pocket?
> Your pickety pockety pocket?
> Early Tuesday morning?
>
> I put in ice cold water
> Nicey icey water
> Slurpy glurpy ice cream
> Early Tuesday morning.
>
> Repeat question: Wednesday morning?
> I put in mashed potatoes

Fluppy gluppy potatoes
Nicey icey water
Slurpy glurpy ice cream
Early Wednesday morning.

Repeat Question: Thursday morning?
I put in sticky molasses
Ickey sticky molasses
... early Thursday morning.

Repeat question: Friday morning?

I put in my five fingers
Funny finny fingers
... early Friday morning
.

It doesn't take long to realize the hardest two words in the whole poem to clean up are "did you."

The second activity is a pronunciation/spelling game. I have all the students stand in a circle and I give each one a 3" x 5" card with a commonly mispronounced word on it. Each card has a companion card; i.e. for-fur, pin-pen, pitcher-picture, feel-fill-fell-file, bead-beat, etc. They are not to let anyone see their card. I call on one student to say his or her word and the rest of the students are to raise their hand when they can spell what they hear. They are not to spell what they think the word is but spell what they hear the student say. Then I ask for the companion word (which many times is mistakenly pronounced with the same sound) and we try to discern the difference in the two pronunciations.

We all become more conscious of our enunciation and pronunciation and tease and remind each other in the midst of conversations and discussions. These games provide a non-threatening fun environment for correcting each other and even the instructor!

*Contributed by: **Harolyn Sharpe** of Florida Community College, Jacksonville, FL.*

Can Learning be a Game?

College professors using jokes in their lectures is not at all new. In fact, just about every profession does it. My church pastor begins every Sunday sermon with a joke. Jokes are good; they usually get the students' attention, make them laugh, and get them in the frame of mind for your lecture. To have students become active participants in class, I believe you need more than a joke; you need an activity. After watching the popular television show *Jeopardy* one night five years ago, I mirrored a classroom activity after that show and am still using it today with enthusiasm. It's a teaching activity that can be implemented within 15 minutes and proves to be quite effective as an event for review or for awarding students extra credit. Either way, the activity produces much excitement and discussion between the students and myself.

Here is how the activity is played for EXTRA CREDIT on a quiz:

1. **Students are asked to respond to ten questions.** The questions may be asked verbally by the instructor one by one or presented to the students typed out on a questionnaire. The amount of time allowed to answer each question is determined by the instructor.

2. **The questions are immediately graded.** Students can exchange papers or, depending on the instructor and class, grade their own. Typically, I will re-read the question and ask a particular student for the answer. It is great to have class discussion at this point, especially if anyone in the class would have a difference of opinion with the answer given.

3. Once all questions have been graded, I ask **that the correct number be recorded in the upper right hand corner of the paper.** These are the students' "playing points."

4. **I announce the final Jeopardy question "category."** Students are asked to wager any amount of playing

points on this question. At this point, the excitement and perplexed look on each student's face is tremendous, as they try to rack their brain, thinking "what do I know or should I know about this topic? They must **write their wager in the lower right hand corner of the paper**—then turn it over.

5. When everyone has turned their paper over, I read the final question. After all answers are written, I ask for the answer. **Correct answers mean that quiz points are added to the wagered playing points and awarded as extra credit. Incorrect answers mean that wager points are subtracted from quiz points to arrive at any extra credit.**

There's no compelling data that a funny presentation is more memorable. The general consensus among professionals I have spoken to, who incorporate entertainment into their presentations, suggests that if students can remember the joke and what it was about or how the game was played, they can often remember the concept within the humor. I know this is true as I have students who at the end of the semester are still talking about that final Jeopardy question and how they should have known the answer. I enjoy hosting *Jeopardy* in my classroom as I'm for anything that will help students remember. The paper and pencil or verbal methods of implementing the game are fine; but if you want to computerize the activity, Gameshow Pro2™ is a fast easy software package to use as a way to create more game shows for classroom learning.

Contributed by: **Cheryl Welch** *of University of Akron, Wayne College, Orrville, OH.*

Applications of Cooperative Learning in the Classroom

Cooperative learning processes may be used in a variety of ways across the curriculum to help groups to develop critical thinking skills, to remain task oriented and accountable, and to benefit from the findings of the subgroups.

Cooperative Learning Communities

Synergy results when students cooperate in the learning process. Students are aware of the synergy in their daily lives. They know that when a group gathers for a common purpose, the energy in the group and the capability of the group creates a stronger, more compelling response than that generated by one person working alone. Additionally, when group members make their own decisions regarding details of a proposed learning outcome, they become stakeholders in the process. Collaborative decision making reflects the effectiveness of the learning community brought together mutually to learn and to share together.

At the beginning of the course, the instructor (as facilitator) may want to clarify how group processes work effectively. Groups should be encouraged to brainstorm without "shooting down" anyone's ideas, to maintain respect for each individual's contribution, to stay on the task, to participate actively, to honor time limitations and to set aside personal agendas.

Pairing or grouping students in dyads has the advantage of heightening accountability. When students learn in pairs, both present the results of their learning to the large group. For example, if each dyad is given a specific question, one student may verbalize the question and answer while the other student substantiates the answer.

In cooperative learning groups of three to five (more than five students in a group may not be as productive), the instructor may want to explain to students the task-oriented and maintenance-oriented functions of group members. Task-oriented functions include those of initiating, seeking information, giving information, clarifying, summarizing, and creating consensus.

Maintenance-oriented functions include encouraging, gate keeping (awareness of distribution of time among group members), setting standards, harmonizing, relieving tension, expressing group feeling.

In a typical group experience, students may be asked to check the appropriate functions as they contribute to the group. Using a checklist may heighten awareness of the cooperative learning process.

Types of Group Process

- **Dividing the Task:** In dividing the task, the instructor assigns part of a larger learning project to each group. Students divide their portion of the project into individual parts. Each student presents the individual findings to the group, which then synthesizes the individual responses into one answer that is shared with the class verbally and visually.

- **Critical Thinking Process:** Each group generates responses to the task together. This is especially beneficial when the objective of the task involves critical thinking questions. Group discussions of this type touch on a variety of answers and examine implications which otherwise might be overlooked. The quality of the responses is more thoughtful through group exchange. As each group presents the rationale for their findings verbally and visually, class discussion illuminates the results.

- **Multiple Options:** When each student is provided with an option of three or four questions on which to write or respond, students may be grouped according to their first preference. Each group then has the same clear goal in which each student is a stakeholder.

Sometimes, as an additional option, it may be useful for students to subdivide the material. After each student has been given sufficient time to generate a thoughtful response, students share answers within the group.

ح **Student Choice:** Students are offered various aspects of a question to explore. In their group, they decide their first and second choices and write these on the board. The class looks at the preferences of each group and decides together how to divide the material.

Reporting Methods

When feasible, large group reporting methods are enhanced when, in addition to an oral report, a visual component is provided. Using an overhead transparency to elucidate how and when an answer was found (especially helpful in providing concrete evidence in problem solving) has the advantage of using both audio and visual learning styles, and students, working together, share accountability.

In small groups, the visual component may be provided as group members take notes on each report. Creative extensions may be provided by students with special talents through videos, slides, etc.

When students are part of the decision-making process and when collaborative/cooperative processes are used, group synergy, critical thinking skills, and success grow, leading students to a heightened awareness of their own untapped potential and empower.

*Contributed by: **Eileen Teare** of Cuyahoga Community College, Cleveland, OH.*

● ●

Communicating with a Branch Campus

One of the most important concerns in managing adjunct faculty is communication. Members of the adjunct faculty may not have educational backgrounds that acquaint them to basic educational knowledge. They are "not around" to hear the latest information on campus; branch campus adjuncts are even farther removed from these informal communication channels. Formalizing communication is essential for adjunct faculty.

We offer the following tips for formalizing communication:

1. **Start with an overview of the teaching role** when interviewing the potential adjunct. Arrange interviews at the branch campus.

2. **Provide an adjunct faculty handbook/manual**; keep extras at the branch campus.

3. **Hold a meeting for all adjuncts prior to the start of each semester.** If the branch campus is close, alternate meeting locations between the branch and the main campus.

4. **During the pre-semester meeting, provide handouts/documents that will assist the adjunct faculty**; remember to leave copies at the branch campus. Include information that pertains to both the main and the branch campuses; distinguish differences in operations between the two locations. Department heads could plan meetings with their adjuncts the same day/evening.

5. **Publish a newsletter and ensure that the newsletter and informational memoranda go to adjuncts as well as full-time faculty.** If the branch campus publishes a newsletter, work with the branch to include items in their publication. Work with the branch campus administration to distribute these documents to all adjuncts. Send documents well in advance. Mail going to the branch campus may not be received as quickly as mail on the main campus.

6. **Utilize e-mail connections if available.** The campus web page could also list items of interest.

Accurate, timely communication can enhance the success of your teaching program. Remember to include "thank-you's" in your communications with the adjuncts. They provide an invaluable service to your campus and to your students.

*Contributed by: **Swen H. DiGranes** of Northeastern State University, Tahlequah, OK and **Jo Lynn Autry DiGranes** of Connors State College, Warner and Muskogee, OK.*

● ●

Distance Education Primer

Distance education technology is redefining the delivery of instruction in higher education. Teaching at a distance was initially introduced with the correspondence course, commonly referred to as independent study. Advances in telecommunications technology have increased distance delivery mediums, which has proven to be beneficial for both educational institutions and the populations they serve. It allows colleges to offer courses using multiple distance learning technologies that expand educational opportunities to learners physically located beyond the institution's traditionally defined boundaries.

Most colleges have distance education programs using synchronous (interactive video, Instructional Television, Desktop Videoconferencing) and/or asynchronous (telecourse, Internet, CD-ROM) technology that supplement pre-existing traditional on-campus, face-to-face programs. A synchronous course meets at a scheduled time but in multiple predetermined locations. With an asynchronous course, the learners don't attend a formal class but can access instructional materials anytime and anyplace as long as a computer or television and videocassette recorder are available. Programs offered using distance education technologies are usually an integral component of the institution's strategic plan or mission. Specialized programs may be developed to serve an industry in the surrounding community like the Michigan Virtual Automotive College for automobile manufacturers or a targeted degree such as Duke's International MBA program. Combining synchronous and asynchronous course delivery offers flexibility and convenience, and increases educational opportunities for distant learners. Flexibility and convenience are important considerations for distant learners as they tend to be "non-traditional" students who are usually older, self-motivated, and disciplined.

Distance education technologies began with asynchronous delivery using broadcast television, referred to as a telecourse. The telecourse is a self-paced learning system that consists of pre-produced videotaped instructional programs integrates with printed materials such as a syllabus, course outline, study guide, textbooks and tests. The videotapes are broadcast on a public television or cable channel at scheduled times that require that the student live in the viewing area. Students can watch the live broadcast or record it with a videocassette recorder.

Asynchronous delivery has evolved to provide the ultimate in flexibility and convenience to the distant learner with the emergence of the World Wide Web as a delivery medium. On-line delivery has the added value of providing much needed student interaction that earlier asynchronous mediums were lacking. Internet courses use computer-mediated tools to provide text-based communication using e-mail, discussion or bulletin boards, and chat rooms. There are numerous on-line courseware products, which integrate these communication tools for course delivery. Due to the accessibility of the Internet, on-line programs are capable of serving new populations of students beyond the traditional boundaries of the educational institution without face-to-face requirements.

Synchronous delivery (Interactive Television, Interactive Video, Desktop Videoconferencing) requires instructor and some students to meet face-to-face at a predetermined time and location while extending the classroom to multiple locations and groups of students. Interactive Television (ITFS) courses have a scheduled meeting time and a live instructor and class-room that is broadcast on a local cable channel. These class-rooms provide one-way video and two-way audio capabilities allowing remote students to call the instructor to ask questions.

Interactive video courses, commonly referred to as a vir-tual classroom, use two-way video and audio classrooms to ex-tend instructions to multiple locations. The instructor and stu-dents are visible using wide screen television or projection which makes interaction possible among the different sites. The class-rooms that use interactive video are fixed predetermined loca-tions based on the technological infrastructure of the institu-tion.

Conversely, desktop conferencing allows two-way video and audio capabilities in the classroom or in the privacy of the student's or instructor's home. The technology uses an instructor-con-trolled teaming system that delivers synchronous interactive courses in the classroom via the Internet.

Similar to the instructor-selection criteria used in traditional courses, faculty chosen to teach distance education courses are first selected from the institution's existing pool of full-time faculty. Adjunct faculty are approached to teach usually after the internal selection process is complete. Instructional tech-nology training and support personnel are available to assist faculty in designing the course. Support is needed from both the technical and curriculum development support staff. Infor-mation on existing processes for both course development and support should be shared with new distance education faculty to facilitate a smooth transition to the new delivery medium.

Teaching courses using any distance education technology requires that new skills be learned or that existing skills be sharp-ened. Faculty will need to develop additional instructional strat-egies for achieving learning objectives. Irrespective of the deliv-ery medium, maintaining consistent multiple forms of interac-tion is important to ensure the success of distance education students. Creating opportunities for various forms of text-based interaction using computer-mediated tools whether student-to-student, student-to-group, student-to-class, or student-to-instructor is important to replicate the traditional classroom experience. Each of these forms of interaction, both textual and videoconferenced, can be facilitated using distance education technology.

Proven competencies for effective teaching at a distance are course planning and organization, verbal and nonverbal presentation skills, collaborative teamwork, questioning strategies, subject-matter expertise and coordination of student activities at field sites (Cyrs, 1997). Course planning and organization involves understanding the different advantages and disadvantages of the delivery medium and its effect on the course design. Faculty who are new to teaching at a distance will want to take advantage of any training opportunities available at various educational institutions. To prepare for teaching the course, they must identify on-site instructional technology support personnel and the services they provide.

The widespread and ever increasing use of distance education technology presents new challenges and opportunities for faculty. It will necessitate that faculty become more familiar with distance delivery medium trends, learn their institution's priorities concerning distance education, and be willing to initiate participation in its associated programs. New skills and instructional strategies will need to be learned or enhanced to be effective in teaching at a distance. Higher education has embraced each new distance education technology medium which has resulted from advancements in the telecommunications industry, from the telecourse to Internet delivery. To be competitive and be in a position to advance the educational institution's strategic goals, adjunct faculty will need to also embrace these technologies.

References

Cyrs, T.E. (1997). *Teaching and learning at a distance: What it takes to effectively design, deliver and evaluate programs.* New Directions for Teaching and Learning. San Francisco: Jossey-Bass Publishers.

Contributed by: **Tinnie A. Banks** *of Lorain County Community College, Elyria, OH.*

●●●

Halving the Paperwork and Doubling the Fun

A concern of adjunct faculty is how to make class interesting, exciting and meaningful while keeping instructor workload to a reasonable level. If you are too tired to correct mounds of papers at night, try this three-step approach. It will keep you and your students stimulated and save you time. It will enable you to reach, and therefore teach, all the students in your course.

As an instructor of educational psychology, I tell my students that in this course they will learn self-direction, a skill that they can carry with them their entire lives. This process minimizes the amount of time it takes to prepare (and later revise) my syllabus while empowering the students and encouraging critical thinking and problem-solving skills. I use the following three-step model which I hope will help you.

First, rather than requiring a standard research report—which takes hours of your time to correct—allow students to produce a project in the form of art, music, poetry, a play, or the more traditional presentation mode of the paper.

For you, this takes away from feeling overwhelmed when a big stack of papers is before you, awaiting correction. It lets you evaluate in a more relaxed mode—on your couch with your feet propped up, watching student-produced videos. You save time by listening to student-produced audio tapes while driving in the car, just be sure to keep a tape recorder in your car to record your comments on each audio presentations.

For the students, their different styles are acknowledged, and they are allowed to express themselves in whatever mode works best for them. They are allowed to showcase their talents. In addition, students like this approach because they are given a choice, and therefore some control, in the class.

Second, have the whole class develop rubrics to be used for evaluation. Encourage them to make the rubrics as specific as possible. Be sure that this evaluation tool can be used for products that are not standard papers. For example, will the rubric work for a piece of art the student has done as well as it will for a standard paper?

Examples of guidelines include:

1. Is there evidence that the material was read/viewed/ listened to and understood?
2. Did the student explain why the material is important to know?
3. Did the student connect the material to previous classroom and outside learning?
4. Does it show good organization and reflective thinking?

For you, this saves time. The process takes one to two hours. These are hours for which you do not have to prepare. Also, because they have developed the rubric, your students are less likely to complain about any possible unfairness in your grading.

For students, this process encourages critical thinking and problem solving, giving them important life skills. They will perform better on their assignments because they really know what is expected of them. After all, they developed the expectations.

Third, use a three-part assessment for the assignment: self-evaluation, peer evaluation, and instructor evaluation. Have students evaluate their own work according to the rubric the classed developed. The student only puts the numeral you have assigned to them (rather than their name) on their product to assure anonymity and objectivity for the next part, review by the peer evaluators. Randomly distribute the products to pairs of students who work together to evaluate two products according to the rubric. Ask the students to make comment give as much feedback as possible. The original author now has the option of redoing the product based on the feedback he or she received from their peer evaluators.

Finally, one week later, collect the finished products for your evaluation. If a student does not wish to re-do his or her product, that is their choice. I find, however, that most students welcome the chance to improve their work before a grade is given, especially when the improvements are easy to fix, such as correcting spelling errors.

For you, correcting students' work becomes easier since you are correcting polished products rather than work which, in the past, became tedious to correct because of myriad mechanical errors (spelling, punctuation, etc.). The peer evaluation process takes approximately one hour—another hour for which you do not have to prepare.

For the students, this process helps them develop better written language skills. They like it because it gives them a "second chance."

The resulting empowerment for this student-chosen curriculum, instruction, and evaluation model demonstrates the importance of student-selected direction. It allows you, as an adjunct instructor, to adapt various learning styles, to reach—and therefore teach—every student in your course. And it makes your job easier and more enjoyable.

*Contributed by: **Rea H. Kirk** of University of Wisconsin-Platteville, Platteville, WI.*

• •

Testing Process

One of the most time-consuming, tedious tasks for a beginning instructor is the preparation, administration, and scoring ᶠ tests. He or she may wonder if there is not an easier way to ˙˙˙ process. Have veteran instructors discovered

" tricks of the trade" which would make the testing process easier? This article will answer some of the questions regarding the preparation, the administration, and the scoring of the test.

The instructor has to make several decisions in planning for testing, such as the following:

❧ When and how often should tests be given?
The approximate number of tests and tentative times for tests should be decided when the course or unit is planned. There should not be too many or too few tests, based primarily on the nature of the course.

❧ What kinds of questions or items should be used?
The types of test items selected must be appropriate to the subject matter of the course. The instructor must consider his or her instructional objectives and the nature of the content covered. It would be wise to use a combination of test types. The strengths and weaknesses of each type should be considered in relationship to the objectives since some formats are less appropriate than others for measuring certain objectives. For a good list of these strengths and weaknesses, see Brown's article in the Fall 1995 issue of *Adjunct Info.*

❧ How long should the test be?
The length of the test will vary depending upon the length of the testing time, the amount of material being covered, and the types of questions being used. Remember, a test should only sample the body of material being tested. Essay questions may be easier to compose than objective-type questions, but they are very time consuming for students to complete and instructors to score. Typically, one essay question may take longer for students to complete than 50 multiple-choice items. In developing objective-type questions, a good rule of thumb is to allow one minute for every two true/false items and one minute for each multiple-choice item. There should be suffi-

cient time for all students to complete the test within the allotted time without feeling rushed. Another consideration in the test length is to design it so that the instructor is able to score the tests and return them within the next one or two class meetings, while the test material is still fresh on the students' minds. The more time that goes by, the less the students care about the questions they missed. Also, if the instructor scores the tests immediately, he or she is able to determine whether the students are ready to move onto new material.

❧ What emphasis should be given to the various aspects of the content?

Emphasis on various areas of content in a test should be in the same proportion to the emphasis in the instructional program. If a instructor spends 30 minutes explaining a principle which he or she considered to be important, then there should be sufficient coverage of the principle on the test. There should be no "trick" questions. The test should not be so easy or so hard that it does not discriminate between those who know the content and those who don't.

❧ In what order should the test items be placed?

The type of question used, the difficulty of the items, and the content should be considered. Each section should be limited to one test type—for example, a section of true/false, then a section of multiple choice, then matching. The arrangement requires fewer directions, and it is easier for the students because they can retain the same mind set throughout each section. Ideally, the test should be arranged from simple to more complex. This arrangement gives the students confidence; otherwise, they may become frustrated if they are given very complex questions at the beginning of the test.

❧ What about the use of tests developed by the

textbook publisher or test bank questions?
It will certainly save a great deal of preparation time
to utilize these sources; however, be sure to use
questions from the test bank which are representative
of the content that has been taught. It is virtually
impossible for any instructor to use a complete publisher-generated test without making at least some
modifications. If students realize that tests are always
publisher-generated, then the motivation to listen to
the instructor will be diminished.

❧ What about an answer key?
A key for the test should be prepared when the test is
developed. If some items have more than one correct
answer, all possible responses should be included. The
test questions should be very clear in meaning; they
should not be misinterpreted by the students. However, despite one's best efforts, students occasionally
misunderstand a question. In this case, the instructor
should be willing to allow alternate answers and not
penalize the students for their answers.

❧ What about the test reproduction?
The test should be reproduced in a very legible form,
keyed at the computer or typewriter, and be free from
typographical errors. Don't crowd the items on the
page. Ideally, instructors should double space between
test items. Allow sufficient space for the students to
provide their answers. In addition, write very clear
instructions for each part. The directions should
indicate what the students are to do, how they are to
do it, and where they should record their answers. It
is very beneficial to indicate the point value of each
question in each section so students can know how to
manage their time.

❧ Must an instructor observe the students during the test?
Yes, it is imperative that instructors always observe

the students as they take the test. There should be no opportunity for students to cheat. Instructors must not leave the room or get so busy at their desk that they are not aware of what is going on. Some instructors prepare scrambled forms of the same tests when students sit close together. As much as possible, make the room conducive to good test taking; for example, adequate light and temperature, quietness, and sufficient work space. Instructors may want to remind students of the remaining time available or write the minutes left on the chalkboard.

❧ What about using Scantron answer sheets and scoring machines?

By all means use these sources if they are available. This process speeds up the grading of the objective part of the test considerably. In addition, many scoring machines can generate an item analysis of the questions. If there is no Scantron available, have students write their responses to the objective questions on an answer sheet. This will speed up scoring considerably, and the instructor may be able to use the tests later without further duplication.

❧ What purpose does an item analysis serve?

Item analysis allows the instructor to determine the effectiveness of each test item. After the scoring of the test has been completed, the instructor should do an item analysis, unless the scoring machine has already done it. Record the number of time each question was missed. If an item is never missed or was missed by everyone, then it serves no purpose. If many students made a perfect score, the test was probably too easy. On the other hand, if a high percentage of the class made a failing score, it was probably too hard. Some experts recommend that instructors make three stacks with their graded test papers—the top one-third, the middle one-third, and the bottom one-third. Compare those questions missed by each group. Occasionally, there may be a question that the poorer students got right but the better students missed. Go back and study the way the test question was written for a clue as to why this happened.

When instructors return the test, students can give them interesting insight into how they interpreted the question or how the wording was confusing. If the instructor collects the test, not ever allowing tests to circulate, this information can be used to revise the test before giving it again at some future date. However, giving the same test year after year is not wise. The same test just doesn't fit as each time one's teaching and class makeup change but it is not necessary to compose a completely new test each time either.

Although the testing process represents a great deal of time, it allows instructors to evaluate the students and to determine if the students have understood the material. Instructors must become skilled in the test construction process since it is so important in the educational environment.

*Contributed by: **Mary Alice Griffin** and **Donnie McGahee** of Valdosta State University, Valdosta, GA.*

Index

A Handbook for Adjunct/Part-Time Faculty and Teachers of Adults, 6th edition, by Donald Greive

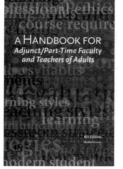

A Handbook carries on the tradition of practical and readable instructional guides.

Intended as a companion book to *Handbook II*, this book is for adjuncts who have already mastered the basics. *Handbook* offers in-depth coverage of some of the topics you just read about like andragogy, collaborative learning, syllabus construction, and testing. But this manual also goes beyond these topics to discuss specific teaching techniques for critical thinking, problem solving, large class instruction and distance learning assignments.

Handbook gives you expert and current strategies to take your teaching to the next level. Available in paperback for $16.00 each.

Teaching Strategies and Teachniques for Adjunct Faculty, Revised 4th edition, edited by Donald Greive and Catherine Worden

This new edition of *Teaching Strategies* keeps the concise format of the previous edition while adding sections on important topics such as:

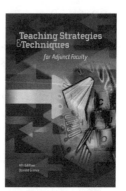

Classroom Teaching Techniques
Out-of-Class Assignments
Instructional Aid Use
Teachnology Use in and out of the Classroom
Evaluation, Testing and Grading

Still the best value for your budgetary dollar, this is a quick and easy reference for adjunct faculty who want to improve their classroom performance. Available in paperback for $10.00 each.

Please go to page 160 to order this and other titles or order online at www.Part-TimePress.com/shop.

Going the Distance: A Handbook for Part-Time & Adjunct Faculty Who Teach Online, by Evelyn Beck and Donald Greive

From technological preparation to course design to planning and virtual classroom techniques, this book offers model materials, practical suggestions and successful strategies. *Going the Distance: A Handbook for Part-Time & Adjunct Faculty Who Teach Online* provides adjuncts who teach in distance education programs with the contents of a first-rate teaching workshop for a fraction of the price. Available in paperback for $13.00 each.

Managing Adjunct & Part-Time Faculty, by Donald Greive, Ed.D. and Catherine Worden

Faculty managers are increasingly challenged by the growth in numbers of part-time faculty. In addition, nontraditional educational delivery systems and entities play a greater role in higher education. The text, written by practitioners, offers the very best in proven management ideas and shares examples of successful and exemplary programs. Topics include:

- Orientation of Adjunct and P/T Faculty Exemplary Models
- The Comprehensive Faculty Dev. Program
- Ethical Issues for Adjunct Faculty and Their Managers
- Legal Issues Concerning Adjunct Faculty and Their Manag
- Distance Ed. Technology: What the Adjunct Manager Needs to Know
- Management of Adjunct Faculty on Branch and Off-Campus Sites
- Evaluation of Adjunct Faculty in a Process for Effectiveness
- Student Retention in Higher Education

Available in paperback/hardcover for $25.00/$35.00 each.

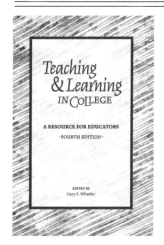

**Teaching & Learning in College:
A Resource for Educators, 4th
edition,** edited by Gary S. Wheeler

The dynamic changes in student and teacher demographics over the past decade suggest that the climate and environment for higher learning has changed. Gary Wheeler of Miami University has assembled six leading educators to present a collection of issues, each offering valuable insight into the state of teaching and learning, targeted at audience of graduate students and relatively new higher education faculty. These are co-authors who can speak authoritatively on topics, but who have also taken the time to personalize the information. Available in paperback for $20.00 each.

Chapters/Topics Include:

Diversity and New Roles for Faculty Developers
by Devorah Lieberman of Portland State University and Alan E. Guskin of Antioch University. What role does diversity play in student learning and faculty development?

Computing the Value of Teaching Dialogues
by Peter Magolda of Miami University and Mark Connolly of the University of Wisconsin-Madison. What role can technology play in helping teaching and learning?

More Than a Thermometer—Using Assessment Effectively
by Catherine Wehlburg of Texas Christian University. As either teacher or student, when and how do you know when or whether things are going well?

The Adjunct Advocate Magazine

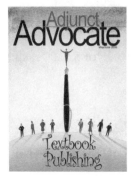

Tens of thousands of temporary faculty call the *Adjunct Advocate* one of the most important professional publications they read and share with their colleagues. *U.S. News and World Report* calls it a "vital resource for the academic community." Here's what each individual subscription to the *Adjunct Advocate* includes:

• Unlimited access online to the current issue and five years of archived issues
• 100 percent satisfaction guarantee (cancel your subscription for any reason, and we'll issue a full refund)

Readers enjoy award-winning writing, including news, reviews of books, journals and new media, interviews, profiles, job and conference listings, as well as calls for scholarly papers/articles. The *Adjunct Advocate* has it all! Treat yourself to a subscription today, and let the *Adjunct Advocate* keep you connected and professionally engaged.

Individual Subscription: $35 per year.

Please go to page 160 to order this and other titles or order online at www.Part-TimePress.com/shop.

FAQ's...

How can I place an orders?

Orders can be placed **by mail** to The Part-Time Press, P.O. Box 130117, Ann Arbor, MI 48113-0117, **by phone** at (734)930-6854, **by fax** at (734)665-9001, and **via the Internet** at http://www.Part-TimePress.com.

How much do I pay if I want multiple copies?

Each of the Part-Time Press, Inc. products has a quantity discount schedule available.

The schedule for *Handbook II: Advanced Teaching Strategies* is:
1-9 copies--$17.00 each   **10-49 copies**--$14.00 each
50-99 copies--$12.00 each   **100 or more copies**--$10.00 each

The schedule for *A Handbook for Adjunct/Part-Time Faculty* is:
1-9 copies--$16.00 each   **10-49 copies**--$13.00 each
50-99 copies--$11.00 each   **100 or more copies**--$9.00 each

The schedule for *Teaching Strategies & Techniques* is:
1-9 copies--$10.00 each   **10-49 copies**--$8.00 each
50-99 copies--$6.25 each   **100 or more copies**--$5.00 each

How can I pay for orders?

Orders can be placed on **a purchase order** or can be paid by **check** or **credit card** (Visa/Mastercard, Discover or AMEX.)

How will my order be shipped?

Standard shipping to a continental U.S. street address is via **UPS-Ground Service**. U.S. post office box addresses go through the **U.S. Postal Service** and express shipments via **UPS-2nd Day, UPS-Next Day**, or **FedEx**. Shipping charges are based on the weight of the shipment, and a fee schedule is shown on the next page. **For international shipping**, please phone 734-930-6854 for rates and carriers.

What if I'm a reseller like a bookstore or wholesaler?

Resellers get a standard **20 percent discount** off of the single copy retail price. No returns allowed.

Part-Time Press, Inc. Instructional Products

Qty	Author:Title	Unit $$	Total
_____	Handbook II	(paperback) $17.00	
_____	Handbook for Adjunct/Part-Time Faculty	(pb) $16.00	
_____	Teaching Strategies and Techniques	(paperback) $10.00	
_____	Managing Adjunct/Part-Time Faculty	(paperback) $25.00 (hardcover) $35.00	
_____	Going the Distance: A Handbook for Part-Time and Adjunct Faculty Who Teach Online	(paperback) $13.00	
_____	Teaching and Learning in College	(paperback) $20.00	
_____	*Adjunct Advocate*: A Journal for Adjunct/Part-time, Visiting and Full-Time Temporary Faculty (**Single 1-yr. subscription**) $35.00		

	Subtotal	
Shipping (See below)		
	Total	

Purchaser/Payment Information

☐   Check (payable to *The Part-Time Press*)
☐   Credit Card #_____   Exp. Date_____
☐   Purchase Order #_____

Name_____   Title _____
Institution _____
Address _____   City/ST/Zip_____
Phone:_____   E-mail: _____

Shipping Fee Schedule:

$0-$30 purchase $6.50

$31-$75 purchase $9.00

Purchases over $75 10% of purchase subtotal

**Mail Form To: PTP, P.O. Box 130117, Ann Arbor, MI 48113-0117
Fax Form to 734-665-9001**